Our Michigan Adventure

by David B. McConnell

09 08 07 06 05 04 03 02 — 12 11 10 9 8

Grade-level Consultants:
Mary Palmer, Robert Palmer

MEAP Consultant:
Rochelle Balkam

Home School Consultant:
Gina Bradstreet

Editorial Consultant:
Eric Keiber

Illustrators:
Theresa Deeter, Don Ellens
Mark Koenig, Robert Morrison
Tim Pickell, George Rasmussen
Aaron Zenz

Computer Graphics and Colorization
Robert Morrison, Aaron Zenz

Film Preparation by Image Arts   *Printing by Friesens*

On the Cover

Michigan is an ongoing adventure! The cover shows images from events and places throughout our history. We have the fireworks of Detroit's Freedom Festival, the beauty of Tahquamenon Falls, the stamina of the French voyageurs, the excitement of the Huron hunter, and the importance of the automobile in our development.

Cover credits: fireworks by David McConnell, Tahquamenon Falls by Nancy Hanatyk, voyageurs in canoe by Theresa Deeter, Oldsmobile car by Ransom Olds, Huron hunter by George Rasmussen. Cover design by Aaron Zenz.

Hillsdale Educational Publishers, Inc.

39 North Street   P.O. Box 245   Hillsdale, Michigan 49242
fax 517-437-0531   phone 517-437-3179
www.hillsdalepublishers.com

Printed in Canada

ISBN 0-910726-39-6

Acknowledgments

Very special thanks to Gina Bradstreet, Eric Keiber, Bob Palmer, and Mary Palmer for taking time from their busy schedules to provide valuable advice. Also, this book could not have been completed without the talents of Aaron Zenz in the area of computer graphics and layout.

It takes many hands to finish a project of this size. My wife and parents have been a great help too, especially my mother. They all pitched in with helpful suggestions.

Additional thanks to Tennille Fenstermaker and the Office of Michigan State Representative Jessie F. Dalman. The many Michigan corporations who provided photos of their operations or products.

My encouragement to all those educators who take the time to present Michigan to their students in spite of a crowded curriculum. Keep up the good work!

About the Author

David McConnell has a lifelong interest in history and teaching. He lives with his wife Janice in their country home near Hillsdale. David has written and developed Michigan studies textbooks and teaching resources for the last 25 years. These include—

Discover Michigan 1981, 1985
Explore Michigan A to Z 1993
Forging the Peninsulas: Michigan Is Made 1989, 1995, 2001
A Little People's Beginning On Michigan 1981, 2002
Michigan Activity Masters 1985, 1999
Michigan's Story 1996, 2002
A Puzzle Book For Young Michiganians 1982

Also served as editor and contributor for
 Computer Games On Michigan, 1996, 2001-2002
 Michigan Student Desk Map and associated 4th grade lessons
 Michigan Government and You
 Michigan Map Skills and Information Workbook

Awards:
Forging the Peninsulas: Michigan Is Made -
   Award of Merit, Historical Society of Michigan.
Discover Michigan -
   Michigan Product of the Year, non consumer division.
Listed in *Michigan Authors* 1993, 2001

CONTENTS

CONTENTS

MICHIGAN Tree of History

1650
1763
1861
1965

The "Tree of History" saw much of Michigan's past. This amazing tree grew from 1600 to 1964. It was growing when the tribes hunted in the woods– when the first Europeans came to Michigan and when the British took control. It was growing when escaped slaves came here to find freedom. It was growing when the first car was driven in Michigan and even when the astronauts went into space. The "Tree of History" grew at East Lansing. The trunk was about 4 feet across. It was 365 years old when it was cut down. You will discover much of what took place during those many years as you read the pages which follow!

Chapter 1   Lesson 1

Meet Michigan

What makes Michigan different than other states in the United States?

Welcome to Michigan. Michigan is full of exciting things. It is an adventure waiting to be discovered! Meet its Indian tribes. Listen to the chief with his great wisdom. March around the old forts where battles were once fought. Sail along with huge ships as they travel the Great Lakes.

Read how the pioneer men and women came here long ago. Learn about their adventures in Michigan. Hear the huge saw buzzing as it cuts our trees into boards. Listen to the put-put-bang of the early cars made here. Meet the women pilots flying a bomber from the factory in World War II!

<u>And of course, it is the state where YOU live!</u>

Our Michigan Adventure

What is Michigan?

Michigan is one of the 50 states of the United States of America. Each state is different than all the others. Have you ever wondered what a state is?

What Is A State?

Land - People - Government

First, a state is an area of land. Each state has its own shape and its own **borders**.

THIS IS MICHIGAN!

Besides the land, a state is the people who live there. You and I are each a little bit of Michigan. The things we do are all a part of Michigan's history too.

When many people come together, they need to make rules to live by. They also need help doing some things. Government is a system of rules and ways to help people. Our government is the third part of what a state is.

Our Shape

Michigan is special because it is surrounded by the Great Lakes. The water of the Great Lakes gives Michigan most of its shape. You can spot Michigan quickly even from outer space. It is the only state that touches four of the five Great Lakes.

THESE ARE THE GREAT LAKES

LAKE SUPERIOR

LAKE HURON

LAKE ONTARIO

LAKE MICHIGAN

LAKE ERIE

The Great Lakes do something special for our climate. They act as a giant air conditioner. In the summer the cool water keeps the air from being too hot. In the winter the lakes keep us a bit warmer.

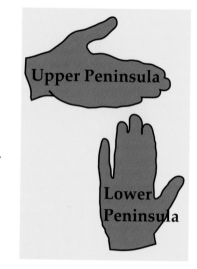

Michigan is the only state divided into two big parts. The northern part is called the **Upper Peninsula**. The southern part is the **Lower Peninsula**. A **peninsula** is land surrounded by water on three sides.

The Lower Peninsula is shaped like a mitten. Some people also say Michigan is shaped like two hands. The Upper Peninsula is the left hand. The Lower Peninsula is the right hand.

Nicknames

Michigan also has nicknames. It is often called "**The Great Lakes State**." Another name is **Water Wonderland** because we have so many small lakes. Then, it is sometimes called the **Wolverine State**. The wolverine is a tough animal that has a bad temper. Probably few wolverines ever lived in Michigan, though.

A WOLVERINE

by Theresa Deeter

4

The nickname Wolverine State started a long time ago. Once the people of Michigan and Ohio argued over the border. They thought it should be moved one way or the other. The people from Ohio started calling the people from Michigan wolverines. They said this because they did not like us. They felt our people were being mean and nasty.

Questions to think about

1. Name the three main things a state is.

2. Tell what you know about the shape of Michigan.

3. Give one nickname for Michigan and tell why it is used.

Brain Stretchers
Make up a nickname for your city. Have it represent something good about your city.

Words In Action!
Imagine you have a pen pal in another country. Write or e-mail a letter to your pal telling about Michigan. Use facts you learned from this lesson.

Chapter 1 Lesson 2

State Symbols

Michigan has many things that are interesting and special. Some of these are seen in our **state symbols** (SIM bols). These symbols remind people of Michigan.

You may wonder how something becomes a state symbol. Usually the state government votes and says so.

The robin became the **state bird** in 1931. It was voted to be the best known and most loved bird in Michigan.

Our **state flower** is the apple blossom. It has been the state flower since 1897. In the spring the apple blossoms are beautiful on the trees.

The tall White Pine is our **state tree**. Many were used for lumber long ago. The lumber helped to build houses here and in other states. Michigan does not have nearly as many White Pine trees today.

The colorful Brook Trout is our **state fish**. It is about eight to ten inches long. Blue, green and red spots cover its sides.

The state symbols are illustrated by Theresa Deeter.

The **state stone** is the Petoskey stone. Many are found on the beaches near the city of Petoskey. This stone is very old. Actually each stone is a piece of **coral**. Coral grows in seas and oceans.

You may wonder how pieces of coral got here. It means we were once covered by a sea! That was a very long time ago. You can see the coral pattern in the stone if you look closely.

In 1973 the state government voted to have a **state gem**. It is the Lake Superior Greenstone. It is green, of course. It is most often found on the beaches of **Isle Royale** (sounds like- eye l roy al). Isle Royale is an island in the cold waters of Lake Superior.

The state soil is called the **Kalkaska** (kal KAS ka) soil. The state government chose this special soil in 1990. This helps people remember how important soil is to all of us. Without soil there would be no farms. We could not grow our food.

Students from Brandywine Elementary School of Niles, Michigan thought Michigan should have a **state reptile**. They asked the government to name one. The students said the painted turtle was the best choice. In 1995 the painted turtle became Michigan's state reptile!

The whitetail deer is Michigan's **state game mammal**. It was made a state symbol in 1997. This idea came from students at Borculo Christian School in Zeeland, Michigan.

The dwarf lake iris became the **state wildflower** in 1998.

Michigan's Flag

Michigan has its own state flag. Have you ever looked closely at one? First, you can see most of the flag is bright blue. In the middle of the flag is the Michigan **State Seal**.

The state seal is a picture which is the official symbol of our state. The seal was designed by Lewis Cass. He was a famous Michigan man of long ago.

The seal has an eagle holding arrows and an olive branch. There is an elk and a moose too. They are next to a shield which has a picture on it. The picture shows a man with one hand raised to mean peace. In his other hand is a gun which means we will defend our state. There is also a rising sun and a lake in the picture.

The seal has several words on it. You probably will not understand these words because they are **Latin** (LAT n).

"E Pluribus Unum"
(sounds like- A PLUR-ih-bus Oo-NUM)
It means "from many, one." It says this because the United States is made of many states.

Another word on the flag is "Tuebor."
(sounds like- TOO-a-bor)
It means "I will defend."

Then there is our **state motto**.
"Si Quaeris Peninsulam Amoenam Circumspice."
(See KWI-rus PINE-in-sul-am AMOY-nam KER-kum-speh-ka)
It means "If you seek a pleasant peninsula, look about you."

Questions to think about
1. List two of the state symbols.

2. What does the Petoskey stone tell us about Michigan a very long time ago?

3. Write the state motto.

Brain Stretchers:
Create your own state flag. Use information that has been discussed or what you have experienced.

Think of another state symbol for Michigan.

Write a new motto for Michigan or your class or school.

Words In Action!
Suppose you could change what is on the state flag. Tell what you would change and why.

The Great Lakes can provide us with many fish if we are careful. People must not catch too many fish. The water must be kept clean. Picture courtesy of the Michgian State Archives.

Chapter 1 Lesson 3
The Water Around Us

The Water Around Us

What makes those funny shapes on the map? Why do our peninsulas look like that? Michigan has its shape because of the Great Lakes around it. You know the Great Lakes divide it into two peninsulas. All the Great Lakes except **Lake Ontario** touch the land of Michigan.

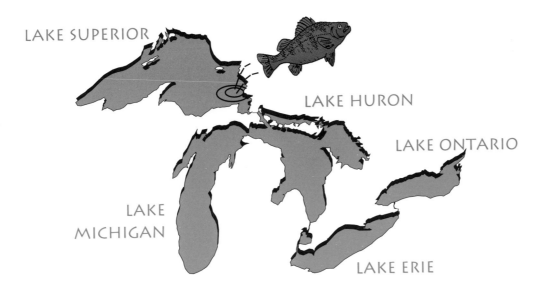

To remember the names of all five Great Lakes, think of HOMES. Each letter in HOMES is the start of one of the Great Lakes.

Lake **H** uron
Lake **O** ntario
Lake **M** ichigan
Lake **E** rie
Lake **S** uperior

Our Michigan Adventure

Superior

Largest and Deepest

Lake Superior is the largest and deepest of the Great Lakes. It is over 1,300 feet deep. Lake Superior is so big it is the largest fresh water lake in the world! Only the oceans and seas filled with saltwater are bigger. Its water is very cold all year. This lake has many shipwrecks. It would be spooky to see one - down in the dark, cold water!

All In The U.S.A.

Lake Michigan is the only Great Lake completely inside the United States. The others are all shared with **Canada**. Canada is another country next to Michigan. There are many great sand dunes on our side of Lake Michigan. Some of them seem as big as mountains.

Michigan

Huron

On the East Side

The French explorers gave **Lake Huron** its name long ago. They named it after the Indian tribe living along the shore. It is the second largest Great Lake. Lake Huron has the most islands, but many of them are in Canada.

Not Very Deep

Lake Erie is one of the smaller Great Lakes. It is between Lake Huron and Lake Ontario. Lake Erie is the most shallow. It is also farther south than the others. Lake Erie only touches a small part of Michigan. Even Lake Erie is much bigger than any lake inside of Michigan.

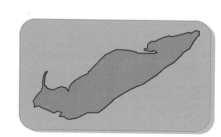

Erie

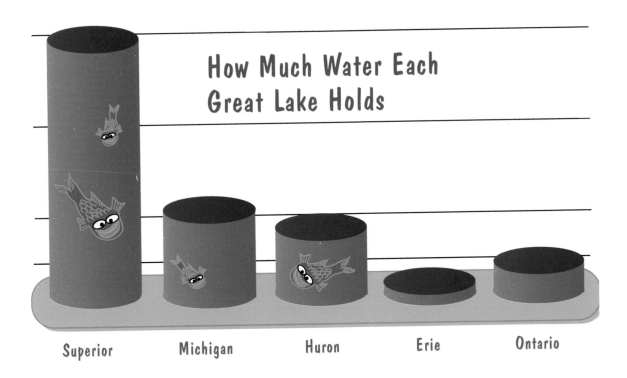

How Much Water Each Great Lake Holds

Superior   Michigan   Huron   Erie   Ontario

Rivers Fill the Great Lakes

How do the Great Lakes get their water? It comes from rain. Some rain falls right into the Lakes.

Other rain falls on the land, but travels into the Lakes. That water flows into the low places. Rivers drain the low places and carry the water away. All Michigan rivers flow into one of the Great Lakes touching our state.

Which Are the Longest?

Michigan's longest river is the **Grand River**. It begins as a tiny creek in southern Michigan. It travels 225 miles to reach Lake Michigan. Along the way it passes through some important cities. The Grand River connects our **capital** city, Lansing, with Grand Rapids, our second largest city.

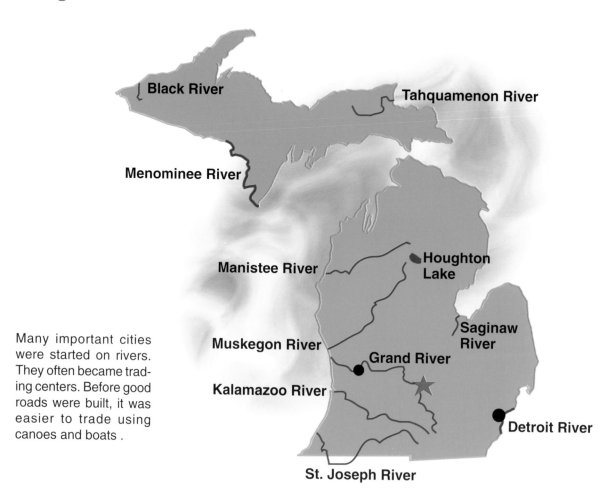

Many important cities were started on rivers. They often became trading centers. Before good roads were built, it was easier to trade using canoes and boats .

Some of the other long rivers in our state are:

Kalamazoo (kal ah mah zoo) River
Manistee (MAN es tee) River
Menominee (meh NOM eh nee) River
Muskegon (mus KEE gon) River
St. Joseph (SAYnt JOE sif) River

The Menominee River is in the Upper Peninsula. It makes part of our border with Wisconsin. The other long rivers are all in the Lower Peninsula. Find them on a map.

The Detroit River is over 2,000 feet wide. That makes it our widest river.

Roaring Waterfalls

The Lower Peninsula has most of the long rivers. The Upper Peninsula has most of the waterfalls. One river- the Black River- has 11 waterfalls by itself. Look for it in the western corner of the Upper Peninsula.

Michigan's biggest waterfall is in the eastern Upper Peninsula. Its name is **Tahquamenon Falls** (tah KWAH meh non). This waterfall has two parts. At the tallest part the water drops 48 feet. The water flows east into Lake Superior.

Courtsey Thomas Schneider and Travel Michigan.

11,000 More Lakes!

There are many small lakes—about 11,000 in all. These lakes are wonderful for fishing and boating.

The biggest lakes inside Michigan are all in the Lower Peninsula. The state's largest inland lake is **Houghton Lake** (HO ton).

Questions to think about:

1. Name the five Great Lakes. Underline the ones touching Michigan.

2. Tell all you can about Michigan's longest river.

3. Which peninsula has our biggest waterfalls?

4. Is this true or false? "Houghton Lake is bigger than Lake Erie."

Brain Stretchers
Compare the size of Lake Superior and Lake Michigan. Make a chart to show the different sizes. (Hint: Trace the two lakes onto paper which has small squares. Count the squares.)

Words In Action!
You are a French explorer seeing Michigan for the first time. Write a journal entry describing what you see here. Tell about the lakes, rivers, land, and people you meet. Use the pictures in this chapter to help give you ideas.

Lake Superior is called the big, bad wolf of the Great Lakes. It can have really rough weather and big storms. Gordon Lightfoot wrote a song about a huge freighter which sank in Lake Superior.

Chapter 1 Lesson 4
Be Michigan Map Smart

Our Neighbors

Can you name the other states that touch Michigan? There are three of them. **Ohio** and **Indiana** touch the bottom of the Lower Peninsula. **Wisconsin** touches the west end of the Upper Peninsula. These are all a part of the **Great Lakes Region**. Since these states all share the Great Lakes, they have much in common. People often think of the land around the Great Lakes as one **region**.

Michigan is next to a foreign country. On a map you can see that this is **Canada**. Canada also shares the Great Lakes with the United States. Canada is north of Michigan and to the east.

Three rivers form the border between Canada and Michigan. To reach Canada you must cross one of these on a bridge. The land of Michigan and the land of Canada do not touch.

Michigan's neighbors.

The Canadian flag

The people of Michigan are friendly with the people of Canada. You can go across the border any time you wish. Many people take vacations in Canada. Also, products are shipped from Michigan to Canada and from Canada to Michigan.

Our Cities With the Most People

Most of the people in Michigan live in cities. Our largest city is **Detroit.** Detroit is in the Lower Peninsula near Canada. Look on your map and find Detroit. About one million people live in Detroit. It is one of the largest cities in the United States. Detroit was started about 300 years ago, but it is not our oldest city.

Michigan's second largest city is **Grand Rapids**. It is in the western part of the Lower Peninsula. Grand Rapids is much smaller than Detroit. About 200,000 people live there. Grand Rapids was started about 170 years ago.

Warren and **Flint** are almost the same size. They are our third and fourth largest cities. They have about 140,000 people each. Pioneers started Warren about 1835 and Flint in 1819. Both of these cities are not far from Detroit. Look on a map and find them. Many of the people in Michigan live in or near Detroit.

The cities in the Upper Peninsula are all smaller than these. In the Upper Peninsula the largest cities are **Marquette** (mar KETT), **Escanaba** (ES can aba) and **Sault Ste. Marie** (soo SAYnt Mar ee). Marquette has the most people. About 22,000 people live there.

Sault Ste. Marie is the oldest city in Michigan. It began in 1668. Wow, that was a long time ago! The second oldest Michigan city, **St. Ignace** (SAYnt IG ness) is also in the **U.P.** It began in 1671. The name Upper Peninsula is sometimes shortened to the letters U.P.

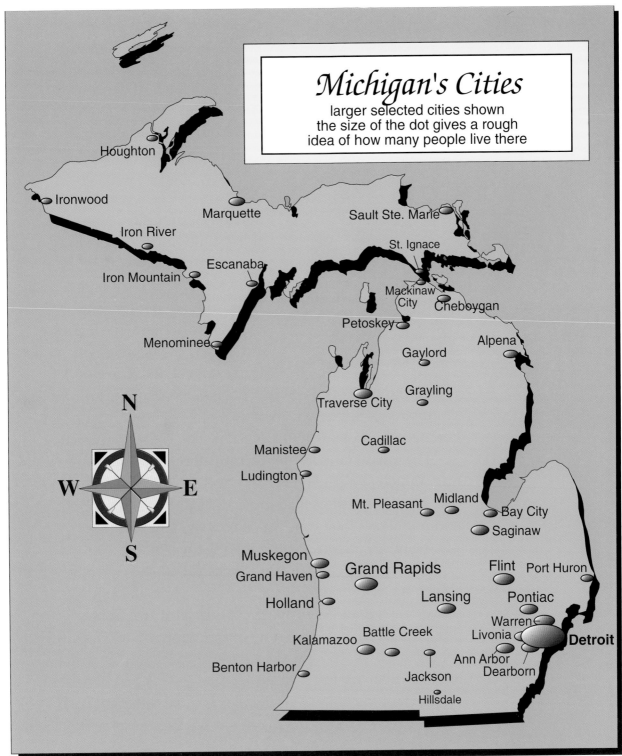

Michigan's Cities

larger selected cities shown
the size of the dot gives a rough
idea of how many people live there

Houghton

Ironwood

Iron River

Marquette

Sault Ste. Marie

St. Ignace

Iron Mountain

Escanaba

Mackinaw City

Cheboygan

Petoskey

Alpena

Menominee

Gaylord

Grayling

N

W   E

S

Traverse City

Cadillac

Manistee

Ludington

Mt. Pleasant   Midland

Bay City

Saginaw

Muskegon

Grand Haven

Grand Rapids

Flint   Port Huron

Lansing

Pontiac

Holland

Warren

Livonia

Detroit

Battle Creek

Kalamazoo

Ann Arbor

Dearborn

Benton Harbor

Jackson

Hillsdale

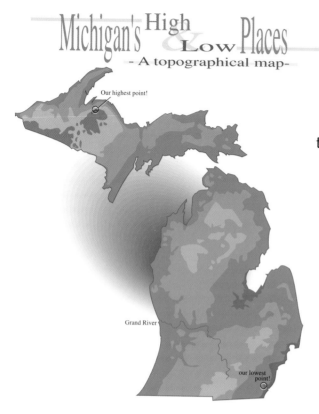

Michigan's High & Low Places
- A topographical map -

Our highest point!

Grand River

our lowest point!

Compare Those Peninsulas

Remember which peninsula has the most land? It is the Lower Peninsula. This peninsula looks like a mitten on the map. It has enough land to make about two and one-half Upper Peninsulas.

The U.P. has some of the oldest cities. The Lower Peninsula has more cities. Almost thirty times more people live in the Lower Peninsula!

The Upper Peninsula has more mountains. The land there is the highest. The highest mountains in Michigan are **Mt. Arvon** and **Mt. Curwood**. Each is almost 2,000 feet tall. They are a part of the Huron Mountains. Another group of mountains in the U.P. are the Porcupines. They are in the western part of that peninsula.

The lowest land in Michigan is along the shore of Lake Erie. Which peninsula has that area?

Two other things the Upper Peninsula has are copper and iron. For a long time much copper came from Michigan's U.P. Iron is still mined there.

The Upper Peninsula is farther north so it is usually colder. It has a shorter season to grow crops. Talk about snow. The Upper Peninsula really has a lot of it. Some parts can have 20 feet of snow in one winter! That is almost enough to cover a house! Most parts of the Lower Peninsula have less than five feet each winter.

Each of Michigan's peninsulas is quite different. Each can be a region by itself. We can say Michigan has two regions of its own. Michigan is also a part of a bigger region- the Great Lakes region.

It Looks Like a Jigsaw Puzzle!

On some maps Michigan might look like a jigsaw puzzle. You can see many squares and other small shapes. Why? Michigan is divided into many **counties**. Most of them look like little boxes on the map. There are 83 altogether. Each has its own name. Keeweenaw County is the farthest north. Wayne County has the most people. Marquette County has the most land.

Other counties are named after different things. Iron County has iron mines. Chippewa County is named after an Indian tribe. Jackson is named after a president of the United States.

Do you know the name of the county where you live? Have someone help you find it on a map. Check to see what other counties touch yours.

A county is like a little state in many ways. Each one has its own capital, called the county seat. That city has a building called the county courthouse. Trials are held in the courthouse. Many records are also kept in the courthouse.

Michigan's 83 counties.

Michigan has many counties. This makes it easier for the people. They do not need to travel far to the courthouse. Driving a long way to go to court or to record a land sale would be a bother. Counties are also small to help meet the needs of the people. People from one area often have different needs than those in another. If our counties were big, it might be hard to please everyone. It would be harder for county government to help all the people.

Questions to think about:

1. Name the three states touching Michigan.

2. Name the two largest cities in Michigan.

3. Compare two things about Michigan's peninsulas.

4. What are two regions inside Michigan?

5. Why doesn't Michigan have just three or four counties?

Brain Stretchers
Compare how many people live in Michigan's two largest cities. Show your work on a graph.

Find the height of the world's tallest buildings. Use an encyclopedia or the internet to help you. Compare their heights to our Mt. Arvon and Mt. Curwood.

Study a Michigan map which shows its counties. Decide which county in each peninsula has the most land .

Words In Action!
Use the Michigan county map. Write about the county where you live. How close is your county to another state? How close is your county to a big city? How close to mountains? What is special about your county?

Chapter 2 Lesson 1

Michigan's First People

How did life change for Michigan's tribes
once they met the Europeans?

Story illustrated by Don Ellens.

An Adventure Begins

Shhhh! Quietly come to the shore of Lake Michigan.
Come to the land of our first people. Step back in time
over 300 years. This is long before your great grandparents were born. Let the years fall away like the crisp
brown leaves of the trees before winter.......

A brother and sister wait along the shore. They are
your age. The cool breeze from the water touches their
faces. Both listen. They wait for the splash of **canoe**
paddles. At first there is only the soft sound of the
waves on the sandy beach. The boy and the girl hide
quietly behind the pine branches. They want to see, but
not be seen. Each is excited and curious.

Who are they? The children are **Native Americans**.
Native means first when used this way. The girl's name
is Gijikens (sounds like- GIJ eh kens), which means
small cedar tree. Those in her family call her Giji. Her
brother's name is Nabek (sounds like- NAY beck) and it
means a boy bear. They are members of the **Ojibwa**
tribe. (Ojibwa sounds like- o JIB wah.) Their home is in
the Upper Peninsula. Since they are young, they have
never seen traders before.

The Traders From Far Away!

Giji says, "Look! They are coming in two very big canoes."

"I can see them too, Giji. Look at them. Their skin is so light. Their faces have much hair. Ha! It looks like they have little bears on their cheeks!"

"**Bonjour** (BOn jzure)," shouted one of the traders to the Ojibwa along the shore.

Giji and Nabek did not know this was a **French** greeting meaning "Good day!"

"Brother, listen. The traders talk so strangely. They speak some of our words, but they say them poorly!"

"Umm, well why not, Giji. I hear those men come from a place very far from here. Their home is across a great water which is even bigger than our own," Nabek said, as he pointed to Lake Michigan.

"Yes, Nabek, Father said it is a place called **France**."

One of the French traders

Such Exciting Things!

The strange traders are taking many things from their canoes.

"Look, Giji. Look what they have! They brought such pretty beads and blankets with bright colors! Father is handing them some of his furs. He caught many muskrat, beaver, and fox last winter. The traders seem pleased."

"What do mother and father want from the traders, Nabek?"

"Father said he wants to trade for one of their long guns. He wants one like the traders use themselves. He will not settle for the cheap ones they bring to trade."

"Oh, Nabek! Look at those shiny metal cooking pots. Mother would really like some of those. They are so much better for cooking than our clay ones."

"The metal pots are nice, Giji. Father also needs some new animal traps and lead balls for his old long gun," said Nabek.

"Don't forget some of the black shooting powder," Giji reminded him.

How Did They Do?

"Well, Giji, mother has her metal pots. She also has two blankets and some metal sewing needles. Mother made a good trade using her sugar from the maple trees. She also traded the **wild rice** she gathered. I don't think father got the trader's long gun, though. He seems a little sad."

"But, Nabek, he has a new metal hatchet. Father also got lead balls to shoot from his gun, more shooting powder, and a beautiful blanket."

Now the traders are loading the furs into their canoes. Giji and Nabek watch as they push away from the shore. The traders begin singing as their paddles dip into the blue water. Soon they are out of sight. Giji and Nabek scurry back to their village.

Later, their father told them he tried to trade for the Frenchman's long gun or rifle. He offered the best furs for it. The trader said he would not give it up except for ALL the furs! Father could not do that. He had to think about the rest of the family too. They would not have any new traps or blankets, if he did. That was just too much to give for any gun.

Things the traders brought.

26

HOW MANY FURS DOES IT COST?

Prices may change without notice!

BLANKET...................... 3 BEAVER OR 4 DEER SKINS
GUNPOWDER .... 1 BEAVER FOR EACH POUND
BRASS KETTLE .... 1 POUND OF BEAVER FOR EACH POUND
60 LEAD BULLETS..... 1 BEAVER OR 15 MUSKRATS
CLOTH .... 1 BEAVER FOR EACH YARD (3 FEET)
EARRINGS .... 1 SMALL BEAVER FOR EACH SET
HATCHET .... 5 BEAVER OR 10 FOX SKINS

Giji and Nabek's father had to make a tough choice while trading. He had the **opportunity** to make the trade. He would pay a cost if he did. When you buy something you must make the same choice. *Do you have to give up too much to get what you want?*

Questions to think about.

1. What country was home to the fur traders?

2. What things did the Ojibwa get from the traders? How did these things make life easier?

3. What were the good points and bad points of trading all the furs for the rifle? List them.

Brain Stretchers
Tell how many beaver furs a French trader wanted for a blanket, two yards of cloth, and two sets of earrings.

Words In Action!
Write about a choice you made when you bought something. What did you give up to make your purchase?

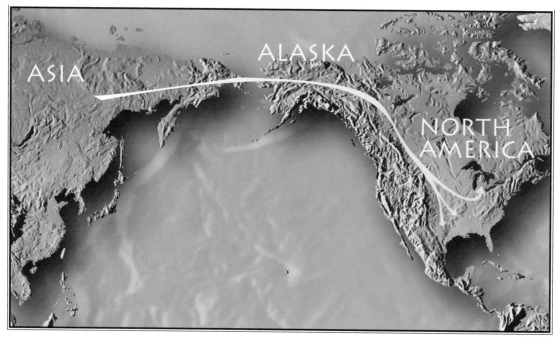

The first people reach Michigan. The gap they crossed from Asia is now called the Bering Strait.

Chapter 2 Lesson 2
From the Beginning

From Where Did They Come?

Scientists believe at one time there were no people living in **North America**. Then from where did the tribes of Native Americans come? It is believed groups moved from **Asia** to **Alaska**. They crossed a strip of land which is now covered by the ocean.

Why did they move? They probably followed the animals which they hunted for food. Maybe they just wanted to explore. After they reached North America, they spread out. Finally, some of them reached Michigan.

These Asian people were the **ancestors** of the Native Americans. Ancestors are relatives who lived before you. Your grandparents are some of your ancestors.

Sometimes Native Americans are called **Indians**. It is because some early explorers were lost. The explorers thought they had arrived in India!

When Did They Arrive?

How long ago did the first people come to Michigan? We think they reached southern Michigan first. That was between 11,000 and 12,000 years ago!

At that time, a great **glacier** covered the rest of the land. The glacier was a giant layer of ice. It was as much as a mile thick!

How do we know these things? **Archaeologists** (are kee OL oh jists) tell us. Archaeologists are scientists who study the way people lived long ago. They often look for clues buried in the ground. They dig up arrowheads, old bones, and other things left behind.

How Many Were There?

When the tribes lived here alone, there were fewer people than today. Probably between 35,000 and 45,000 Native Americans lived in Michigan before the French came. Today almost ten million people (10,000,000) live here!

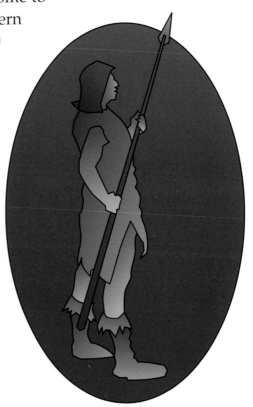

The first people who lived in Michigan probably came here 11,000 to 12,000 years ago.

Names of the Tribes

Giji and Nabek are **Ojibwa**. They want you to know more about their tribe. The word Ojibwa means a kind of moccasin- like the ones that tribe wore. Really this is a name used by neighboring tribes. The Ojibwa called themselves **Anishnabek** (ah NISH na bek). It means first people.

Each tribe had a word in its language meaning "the people " or "first people." That is the name they usually call themselves.

Do Not Be Confused

The names of tribes often have different spellings. This is because most tribes did not have written words. People heard the same word but often spelled it differently. Ojibwa is the same as Ojibway or even Chippewa. They all mean the same tribe.

Giji and Nabek's
Villiage

N
W E
S

The Ojibwa

Nabek says, "Our tribe is a large one. Our tribe does not just live in Michigan. We live all across the northern Great Lakes. But almost all tribes have moved from place to place. Our people have also lived in other places at different times."

Moving with the Seasons- It is for the food

The Ojibwa had summer and winter homes. They did this so they could best use their sources of food. In the spring and summer the Ojibwa lived along the Great Lakes. Nabek enjoyed fishing with his father. They went out on the lakes in their **birchbark** canoe. It

A Native American boy in his canoe gathers wild rice. Courtesy Michigan State Archives.

was nice to be on the cool water during a hot summer's day. Often it was easy to catch a large number of delicious fish.

Giji joined the other girls and women gathering blueberries, cranberries, and raspberries. They might plant some pumpkins, corn, and squash too. She enjoyed seeing how fast the squash and pumpkins grew near the end of summer.

Wild rice was another important food. It grew in swampy areas around lakes. Both Giji and Nabek would go out in a canoe to harvest the rice. Nabek would paddle through the tall rice. Then Giji pulled the plants over the canoe and shook them. The dark ripe grains of rice fell into the canoe.

A wooden corn grinder. Art by Aaron Zenz.

Spreading Out for Winter

During winter each Ojibwa family left the village and went out on its own. Hunting was an important way to get food in the winter. It was hard to find animals if many people hunted in one place. That is the reason the Ojibwa spent the winter in small groups.

When Giji and Nabek were very young, winter was an adventure. They thought the early snow was fun. Nabek and Giji played **snow snake** with other children.

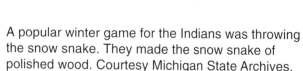

To play snow snake, a long narrow area of snow is packed down. Each player sees who can slide a long smooth stick the farthest. Maybe they also threw snowballs, just as we do today!

A popular winter game for the Indians was throwing the snow snake. They made the snow snake of polished wood. Courtesy Michigan State Archives.

Winter Could Be Tough

As they grew older, children realized winter was not always an easy time. It was harder to hunt in the deep snow. Food became **scarce**. They might get sick because there was not enough to eat.

Giji remembered one hunter. He was very thin and weak when he stumbled back to camp. He told everyone how he survived when he could not find food. He chewed the inside bark of trees!

Wigwams were used by the tribes in Michigan. They were often covered with birchbark. They are still very cold in the winter. Art by David McConnell.

Thank You for Spring!

Wow! Spring! That was a time of great excitement and relief. Warm weather meant more to eat. It was also the time to make maple sugar!

The families went into the forests to collect **sap** from the maple trees. They boiled away the water in the sap. Finally it became maple syrup or maple sugar. The warm sticky maple sugar was such a treat! The tribes used maple sugar and honey to make their food sweet.

Maple trees can live to be two hundred years old. Maybe your maple syrup came from the same tree used by an Indian!

In the springtime Indians collected the sap from the Sugar Maple trees. They often used birchbark containers. Art by Aaron Zenz.

Questions to think about

1. Where did the first Michigan people come from?

2. How long ago did the first people reach Michigan?

3. What does the word Anishnabek mean?

4. What does scarce mean? What became scarce for the tribes in the winter months?

Brain Stretchers
Make a chart or graph to compare how many people lived in Michigan at two times.
1.) when the tribes lived here alone
2.) how many people live here today.

Words In Action!
Imagine you are an Ojibwa boy or girl from long ago. Make up a story about a day in your life.

Chapter 2 Lesson 3
Other Tribes

Who were Giji and Nabek's neighbors? The Ojibwa shared the land with other tribes. There were three main tribes here and smaller ones also.

The Tribes in 1760

Houghton

Ojibwa (also called Chippewa)

Marquette

Sault Ste. Marie

Menominee

Ojibwa or Chippewa

Menominee

Ottawa

Traverse City

no tribe here

Saginaw

Grand Rapids • Flint

Lansing

Potawatomi

Detroit

Battle Creek
Kalamazoo

Huron

Miami ©1997 Hillsdale Educational Publishers

This map shows the areas used by the tribes living in Michigan about 1760. Remember, the tribes moved from time to time. The boundaries often changed.

The Ottawa (OT ah wah) or Odawa. A tribe of the northwest Lower Peninsula.

The Ojibwa and Ottawa were related. Many of their **customs** or ways of living and doing things were also alike.

Ottawa comes from the word "adawa" or "adawe" which means to trade. The Ottawa traded corn, sunflower oil, and tobacco with other tribes.

Each tribe traded something found or grown in its area for something which was scarce. A Michigan tribe could trade copper for a western tribe's buffalo robe.

Once the Ottawa had lived to the east in Canada. They were forced to leave that area by a war with the fierce **Iroquois** tribes. (The "s" is silent in

Iroquois. It sounds like EAR a quoy.) The Iroquois group lived far to the east around Lake Ontario.

Moving to avoid war is one reason for tribes to **migrate** (MY great). A group of people migrate when they move to start homes in a new area. They do this because of some important reason which concerns all of them. They may migrate to find food, or water, or to escape war or disease.

The Potawatomi (POT a WAT o me) A tribe of the south.

The Potawatomi had settled in southern Michigan by the 1750s. The Potawatomi name comes from Ojibwa words for fire. It probably means "people of the place of the fire." They got this name because they burned the grassland before planting their crops.

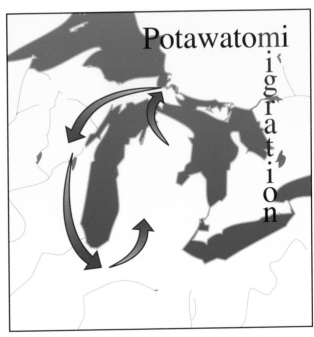

The tribes of the Great Lakes region did not stay in one location. This map shows the movement of the Potawatomi tribe over some 200 years. Map by Aaron Zenz.

35

This tribe lived farther south than the Ojibwa and Ottawa. Since they lived in a warmer area, the Potawatomi could depend more on farming. They planted corn, squash, beans, tobacco, melons, and sunflowers.

Because of their crops, the Potawatomi did not move their villages often. They did not need to find food.

The Potawatomi tribe is related to the Ojibwa and Ottawa. Since these three tribes are related, they are sometimes known as the "**Three Fires**." The three tribes all spoke a language which was similar.

The Three Fires were the main tribes living in Michigan by the middle 1700s. They were not the only tribes though.

Other Tribes

Menominee (meh NOM eh nee)
   A tribe of northern Michigan.

Miami (my AM ee) A tribe of southwestern Michigan.

Huron (hYOUR on) A tribe of the southeastern Michigan.

The **Menominee** tribe lived in the middle part of the Upper Peninsula. The Menominee River is named for them. Their name is an Ojibwa word for "wild rice people." Wild rice was an important food for them. Their customs were much like those of the Ojibwa who lived nearby.

The **Miami** lived in the Lower Peninsula near Niles. Their tribe did not have many people. Their area did not include much of Michigan.

One of the first tribes the French met in Canada was the **Huron** Tribe. They became good friends and traded furs. The tribe actually called itself Wendat or **Wyandotte** (WY n dot).

Later, the Iroquois tribes attacked the Huron forcing them to migrate. The Huron tried different places in Michigan for a new home. They moved near Mackinac and finally near Detroit.

This tribe spoke a language which was different from those of the Three Fires. They also had a different kind of home. The Three Fires tribes lived in wigwams, but the Huron lived in **longhouses.** Longhouses were larger than wigwams. Several families lived in each one. The Huron sometimes built walls around their villages. They made their villages into small forts.

All tribes in the Great Lakes area lived in the forests and woods. Because of this, they are also called **Woodland Indians.**

A Huron longhouse. Art by Tim Pickell

Questions to think about

1. Which tribe lived in your part of the state during the 1700s? Tell something about it. If no tribe lived in your area, choose one to write about.

2. Explain how the tribes living in Michigan were alike or had the same customs. Tell how they were different or had different customs.

3. What does the word migrate mean? Why did some tribes migrate?

Brain Stretchers

Draw a map showing Michigan's tribes. Use your left hand as a guide to make the two peninsulas. Show where each tribe lived. Be sure to label your map.

Words In Action!

Explain which tribes are in the Three Fires group. Why are these tribes put together as a group?

Time line

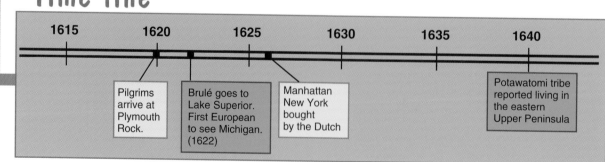

| 1615 | 1620 | 1625 | 1630 | 1635 | 1640 |

Pilgrims arrive at Plymouth Rock.

Brulé goes to Lake Superior. First European to see Michigan. (1622)

Manhattan New York bought by the Dutch

Potawatomi tribe reported living in the eastern Upper Peninsula

Chapter 2 Lesson 4

What Was Life Like for the Tribes?

How the Work Was Divided

The women did certain jobs in the Indian village and the men did others. The tribes in Michigan were alike in many ways. Most of the things men and women did were the same for each tribe.

The men were often away from the village hunting. The women did the work in and around the village. Every job was important and necessary for survival.

What the Women Did.......
Food

Walk to an Indian village at meal time, smell the meat roasting over the fire. Choose from cooked deer, fish, rabbit or squirrel. After dinner, the girls and women would be glad for your help. Pound dried corn into flour using a hollow log or big flat stones. Or you might bring a large deerskin bag of water from the river.

The Indian village at supper time. Art by Aaron Zenz.

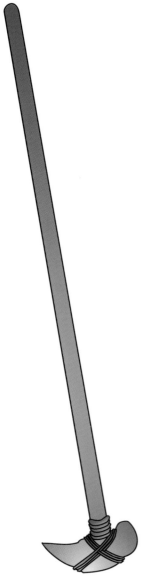

A digging stick used by the tribal women for planting crops. Art by Aaron Zenz.

Clothes

Let the women show you how to clean and skin the animals. Learn how to treat the hides so they would not rot and smell. A lesson making clothes and moccasins from the hides might be interesting.

If there was sewing to do, you might use a bone needle. Thread might be made from plant fibers.

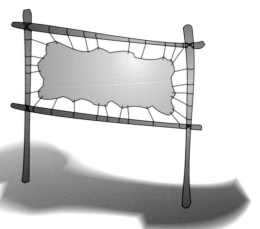

Native American women were skilled at drying and tanning animal skins which they used for clothing. Art by Tim Pickell and Aaron Zenz.

Gardens and Farming

If the tribe planted gardens, the women and girls cared for the crops. The girls kept the deer and rabbits from eating the tender green sprouts. They pulled weeds on hot summer days. Young girls made sure the crows did not eat the corn before it could be picked.

Making Containers

The Native American women were very skilled in making containers. They made clay pots used for cooking. They also made many kinds of baskets. Reeds and strips of smooth tree bark were woven into baskets. Berries and maple sap were gathered in birchbark containers.

A small porcupine quill box.

The tribes got all their food from nature. Some of their meat came from deer. Original art by Frederic Remington, colorized by Aaron Zenz.

What the Men Did.......
Hunting

The men hunted, made hunting tools, and traded. If they didn't hunt or fish most of the time, their families could starve. This was hard work. Often a hunter must walk or go by canoe long distances. Imagine sweating and straining to carry a 150 pound deer back to your village.

Hunting was also dangerous. Suppose a big black bear chased you through the woods? Each second you run faster and faster. You push through bushes and stumble over logs to get away. Wow!

Fishing

Fish was a major food of most tribes. The Indians fished in the summer and on cold winter days too.

An exciting way to fish was at night from canoes. The men and boys carried big torches. The torch light made the fish curious. They swam near the surface and were easier to spear.

The fish was often dried and smoked over a fire to keep it from spoiling. Other kinds of meat were dried and smoked also.

A torch used for fishing at night. Art by Aaron Zenz.

41

Building to Survive

The Native American men made homes, tools, and canoes. It was the men's job to make the bows and arrows. It is quite hard to make good bows and good arrows. For thousands of years the men made their arrowheads chipped from stone. Can you imagine how many hours that took?

Many old arrowheads made of chipped stone are found in Michigan. The stone used for arrowheads is called flint.

Homes

Most tribes needed homes which could be moved or built quickly. The **wigwam** was perfect for this.

The wigwam looked like a big upside down bowl with a door. It had a hole in the top to let out smoke from the fire. Wigwams were usually covered with tree bark. A frame of small bent trees held the bark. The wigwam had one room where the family could eat, sleep, and meet together.

The Indians took saplings or young trees and bent them into a dome shape. Then they covered them with strips of birchbark. The strips could be rolled and carried when they moved.

Warriors

The strong younger men acted as warriors to protect their villages. Sometimes these men went far away to fight another tribe. Some carried deadly war clubs and leather shields. They hoped the shields would protect them from the enemies' sharp arrows and spears.

When fighting their enemies, some tribes used war clubs and shields covered with hide. Art by Aaron Zenz.

Is There an Easier Way?

The Native Americans used food and materials close by. This made them **self-sufficient**. This means they did not need to get things from other people. They could take care of themselves. It is good to be self-sufficient. Still, you can see why the Indians wanted to trade with the French. Metal pots, needles, thread, and blankets from the traders made life much easier.

Questions to think about.

1. What did the Michigan tribes call their homes? Describe one or draw one.

2. Make two lists. On one, write the jobs done by Michigan's Indian women long ago. On the other, write the jobs done by the men. Choose one job you would like to do and tell why. Choose another you would not want to do and tell why.

3. Are most people today as self-sufficient as the tribes from long ago? Explain your opinion.

Brain Stretchers
Make your own recipe for a Native American food. Tell how much of each item is needed. Give directions how to make the dish.

Words In Action!
Tell about how long it might take to fix a Native American meal as done long ago. Tell how long it takes to make a meal today.

Chapter 2 Lesson 5
Gifts From The Tribes

Do the tribes of long ago touch our lives today? Yes they do. They left us many things we use even now.

Art by George
Rasmussen.

Story Telling

The Michigan tribes left us many interesting stories from long ago. For hundreds of years Native American storytellers spoke of **Hiawatha** (HI eh WA tha). They told about him in their **legends** as they sat around blazing campfires.

Hiawatha was strong, brave, and wise. He had magical powers too. His name means "he makes rivers." In some legends, Hiawatha taught how to plant crops. In others he explained how to heal the sick.

Food and Crops

The next time you bite into a warm buttery ear of corn, think about the Indians. They were the first to grow it. Sometimes Indian corn is called **maize** (MAZE). The corn the tribes grew had smaller ears and smaller kernels than our corn does.

An Indian food some people still eat is called **succotash** (SUK oh tash). Succotash is a mixture of corn and lima beans.

There would be no pumpkin pie without the tribes. Corn, pumpkins, squash, and some kinds of beans were first grown by the tribes. Tobacco was first used by the Native Americans. Tobacco was new to the French when they first came.

Inventions

Have you ever been in a canoe paddling down a rushing river? The canoe is a Native American invention. Michigan's first people spent years learning how to make them just right.

When the heavy snow fell, the Native Americans invented a way to walk over it! The **snowshoe** lets people walk on top of the snow.

A second invention for the winter is the **toboggan**. Today the toboggan is used for having fun going down snow-covered hills. The Indians also used this invention for work. It let them move their belongings easily over the snow.

The tribes used the bow and arrow, but this was invented in other parts of the world too.

Snowshoes, invented by the Indians, make walking on deep snow much easier.

Where Did Those Names Come From?

Did you know the Native Americans gave us the name for our state? The word Michigan comes from the words, "michi" and "gama." They mean great lake or big water.

The names of many other places in Michigan also come from Indian words. **Mackinac Island** (MACK in aw EYE land) is one. Mackinac is taken from a longer word meaning great turtle. The Native Americans believe the island looks like a giant turtle swimming across the water. Mackinac Island is between our two peninsulas.

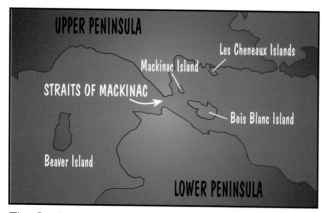

The Straits of Mackinac was a center for fur trading for many years.

The area of water dividing the peninsulas is called Mackinac too. Actually, it is the Straits of Mackinac. **Straits** means a narrow area of water. Look at a map. You can see this is where Lake Michigan and Lake Huron join.

Several Michigan cities have Native American names. Here are some examples:

Kalamazoo (kal ah mah zoo)
Menominee (meh NOM eh nee)
Muskegon (mus KEE gun)
Pontiac (PON tee ak)
Saginaw (SAG en aw)

Kalamazoo means boiling water. The tribes named it after the rushing water in the nearby river. Menominee is the name of a tribe from the Upper Peninsula. It means rice gatherers. Muskegon comes from a word for marsh. The city of Pontiac is named for a chief. Saginaw is named after the Sauk tribe. Our state would not be what it is today without the Native American tribes.

Visitors From Far Away

For thousands of years the Native Americans lived by themselves. They hunted and fished and made everything they needed.

Then about 350 years ago the first people from **Europe** made their way to Michigan. These people came

across the Atlantic Ocean in sailing ships. They came from countries like Britain and France. They kept moving west until some of them reached Michigan. What a surprise for the tribes to see these people who were very different.

Because of the French traders, there were great changes for the tribes. The tribes traded for more and more things. As the trading grew, so did the number of French people living here. Life for the tribes would never be the same again! They became less self-sufficient. People from Europe wanted their land. The tribes became involved in wars between the **Europeans**.

Questions to think about.

1. Tell which Indian invention you believe is the best and why.

2. Find your city or town on a map of Michigan. Look for nearby places which seem to have Indian names. They can be cities, rivers or lakes, etc. Make a list of these names. Try to find what some of the names mean.

Brain Stretchers
Make a time line using centuries. On the time line show these two things:

When the Native Americans started to live in Michigan. When the first French people reached Michigan

Words In Action!
Write your own Native American legend about Michigan.

France

Chapter 3   Lesson 1

Explorers From Far Away

What really attracted the Europeans to come to Michigan
and why did they stay?

First the French, Later the British
The French were the first **Europeans** to visit
Michigan. Europe is a region across the Atlantic Ocean.
It has several countries. Britain, France, Germany,
Holland, and Spain are in Europe.

The French came here to trade furs with the tribes of
Michigan. They also came to explore. They wanted to
find a way to sail to **China**. They thought it might only
be a short distance west of the Great Lakes.

Why Did They Come?
In Europe furs and spices were scarce. They did not
have any **silk** to make fine clothes. America had the

The first Europeans to
visit Michigan traveled
from France. They hoped
they could reach China.
They did not realize it was
so far away.

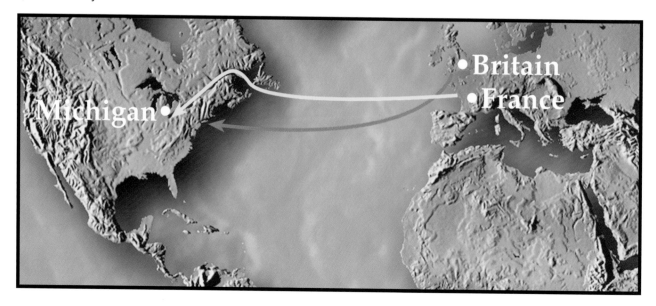

animals for fur. Furs could be shipped back to France and sold for a higher price. China had silk and spices. Those could be sold in France too. This is why the French wanted to find a shortcut to China.

Traveling from France to China was a very, very long trip. Looking for a shortcut to China, the French explored the lakes and rivers. They kept exploring towards the west.

At first the French explored along the **St. Lawrence River** (SAYnt LOR ents). They used this big river like a highway. Their forts and first towns were started along it.

The St. Lawrence River was the pathway which brought the first Europeans to Michigan.

As fur traders and explorers came, so did **missionaries** and **priests**. The missionaries and priests did not come here to make money. They wanted to tell the tribes about God. Missionaries lived with the tribes in far away places. They learned to speak the languages of the tribes. They learned how the tribes lived and their customs.

Those are the three reasons the French came here. They came to explore, to trade furs, and to tell about their God.

The Land Is Ours Now!

Soon the French claimed the land of Canada and the Great Lakes. They said it all now belonged to France. They called this land **New France**. Of course, they ignored the rights of the tribes.

The First Frenchman- We think!

Brule' may have looked like this. There is no known picture of him. He was probably the first European to visit Michigan. Art by David McConnell.

There was a young man named **Etienne Brule´** (ay TYEN broo-LAY). He lived in one of the first villages along the St. Lawrence River. That was in Canada. Brule´ had a wild and thrilling life. He often joined Indians on long canoe trips. Young Brule´ wanted to see where the rivers went. Maybe he could find China!

Historians believe Brule´ was the first French explorer to reach Michigan. It was around 1620 when he came here. He visited the shore of Lake Superior along the Upper Peninsula. Little is known about what Brule´ did because he did not read or write. He only returned to his village now and then.

Don't Go That Way!

When Brule´ canoed west, he did not use Lake Ontario or Lake Erie. The Iroquois tribes lived along those lakes. The French and the Iroquois had become bitter enemies. Once the French helped another tribe fight the Iroquois. The Iroquois never forgave them.

The French had to find another way to go west. So they canoed up the Ottawa River. The Ottawa River took them into northern Lake Huron. This is why the French reached the Upper Peninsula first.

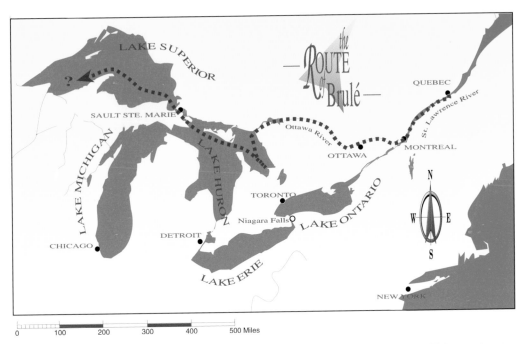

The French explored the land along the St. Lawrence River into the Great Lakes. This was long ago. The explorer Champlain started a village at Quebec in 1608. (Quebec sounds like: KAY bek.)

Questions to think about

1. The French came to Michigan for three reasons. Which reason would not make them any money?

2. About how many years ago did the French first find the land we call Michigan?

3. Explain why scarcity caused the French to travel to Michigan.

Brain Stretchers
How many miles is it from Michigan to China?

Words In Action!
Brule´ has just returned from an exciting exploration. What questions would you ask him about his journey?

Chapter 3 Lesson 2

A Brave Priest in a Strange Land

Let's find out about one of those early French missionaries, **Jacques Marquette** (jHAK mar KETT). He is sometimes called Pere (peer) Marquette. Marquette was born in 1637 to a respected family in northern France. When he was 17, he decided to become a priest. He studied long and hard for this work, finishing his studies in 1666.

Names Used for Marquette

Jacques Marquette was a French priest. He belonged to the Catholic church. Priests are called "Father" out of respect. This is why in some places you may read about Father Marquette instead of Jacques Marquette. The word father in French is "pere." Thus, certain people will say Pere Marquette. The river in western Michigan is the Pere Marquette River. That is another way of saying the "Father Marquette River".

Father Marquette's greatest wish was to become a missionary in America. He wanted to bring his **religion** to the tribes. The missionaries who went to America were heroes in France. Some of them had been killed by the Indians. Imagine traveling so far to a strange land. It might be like traveling to the moon today!

At last Marquette was sent to Canada. After several months, he traveled to our Upper Peninsula and studied the Ottawa and Huron languages.

Michigan's First Two Towns

Marquette started two **settlements** with little churches. That was over 300 years ago in 1668 and 1671. These were at **Sault Ste. Marie** (soo SAYnt-ma-REE) and **St. Ignace** (SAYnt IG-nes). These towns are in our eastern Upper Peninsula. He started the two oldest towns in Michigan!

Many among the Ottawa and Huron tribes became Christians because of his work.

Jacques Marquette started the settlement of Sault Ste. Marie. This is Michigan's oldest city. Courtesy Michigan State Archives.

To Explore a Big River

Marquette knew a young fur trader named **Louis Jolliet** (loo ee ZHOL-ee-ay). In 1672, Jolliet asked Marquette to come with him. He was going to explore a great river. This was the **Mississippi River**. Marquette could speak to the tribes on the way. No Europeans had traveled down this river. They would be the first ones.

In May of 1673, they left St. Ignace to begin their adventure. They paddled along the north shore of Lake Michigan to Green Bay, Wisconsin. Along the way they stopped at a village of the Menominee tribe.

Please Don't Go!

When they said where they were going, the Menominee gave them a stern lecture. They said something like this:

There are tribes who are mean to strangers. They break their heads without any cause. There is even a monster, whose roar is heard from a great distance. This monster blocks the way and will swallow up anyone who comes too close!

Marquette told the Indians he could not take their advice. He said his work was so important, he would risk his life.

The Indians Helped Them

Marquette and Jolliet took their canoes up the **Fox River** in Wisconsin. Another Indian village was sighted. They asked if two guides could help them. They wanted to find a river which flowed into the "Mesippi" (Mississippi).

On June 10, the Frenchmen and two guides left. An amazed crowd of Indians watched. They paddled through swamps and many small lakes. Marquette wrote:

*"We greatly needed our two guides, who safely conducted us to a **portage** of 2,700 **paces**, and helped us to transport our canoes to enter the river; after which they returned home, leaving us alone in this unknown country...."*

Alone In Dangerous Country

Now the men went down the **Wisconsin River.** Marquette wrote this in his diary on June 17th. "We safely entered the Mississippi... with a joy I cannot express."

What did they see in the new land? There were no Indians, at first. Still, they worried about unfriendly tribes. At night the men slept in the canoes in the river. Eight days later, they saw footprints along the riverbank! Marquette and Jolliet followed the footprints.

They shouted and yelled to attract the Indians- and maybe end their lives! Marquette spoke to them in the language of the Illinois tribe. Would they understand? Yes, they did! Soon, as was the Indian custom, pipes were smoked as a token of peace.

Time to Go Back

Marquette and Jolliet then continued on their journey. After several days, they were sure the Mississippi did not go to the Pacific Ocean. It carried the explorers further and further south. This river was not a way to China! The two men had followed the Mississippi for over six hundred miles. They decided to turn back toward home.

The trip had been very hard and Marquette became ill. Jolliet left Marquette at an Indian village on the Fox River. Maybe he could rest and get better, but his illness lasted over the summer. Still, he returned to visit the Indians in Illinois.

Marquette Was Very Sick

There his illness grew much worse. Two French friends came to help him back to St. Ignace. The friends paddled hard and fast. Sadly, Marquette did not make it. One night he died along the shore of Lake Michigan.

The year was 1675. His friends buried him near a river. Now this river is called the Pere Marquette in his honor.

Marquette was a brave priest. Many priests and missionaries worked hard to tell the tribes about their religion.

Father Marquette died on the sand dunes near the Pere Marquette River. The river was named for him. Art by Aaron Zenz.

Jolliet Had Trouble Too

What happened to Jolliet? He had almost reached his home in Canada. Then he and his men went through a terrible **rapids** on the St. Lawrence River. The canoes flipped over and were smashed. Some of the men drowned.

Poor Jolliet lost all his notes about the trip. One of the canoes was borrowed from his sister-in-law. She was upset when Jolliet could not return it. Then she sued him in court. What a way to end a great adventure!

Questions to think about

1. Use geography terms and compass directions to explain the path the Mississippi River takes.

2. Make a time line of Jacques Marquette's life.

3. Where were the first two French settlements in Michigan?

Brain Stretchers:

Use a map and find out how far Jolliet and Marquette traveled from St. Ignace to the place they joined the Mississippi River.

Words In Action!

Imagine that you are Marquette or Jolliet. Write a letter to your family in France telling about canoeing from St. Ignace to the Mississippi. What did you see on your journey? What were your hardships?

Compasses help tell direction

Chapter 3 Lesson 3
More About Maps and Globes

The French explorers needed maps. A good map was very valuable to them. They had to learn where to go in this big, new land. Maps and globes may seem like mysteries to you. It is time to learn about the things maps and globes can tell you.

Use the Map Clues

What clue tells you which way is north? Almost all maps have labels for north and south. North is usually at the top and south is at the bottom. The map maker may write the words "north" and "south" on the map. That makes it easy! Some maps may have an "N" for north and an "S" for south.

Other maps may have a picture of a **compass** printed on them. The printed compass on your map will also point to the north.

A real compass is a device with a pointer. It points toward a magnetic place on the earth. This place is far to the north, so a real compass points north. People use compasses to know the direction they are traveling.

The Main Directions and Others

There are four main directions: north, south, east and west. There are four directions in-between those: northeast, northwest, southeast and southwest. Map compasses may not always show those in-between directions. Understand how to find them on your own.

Lines All Over My Map!

Most maps and globes have several straight lines. Some of these go across, and some go up and down. These lines help you find other places on the map.

The lines of **latitude** (LAT i tude) go across from side to side. Here is an idea to help you remember latitude. Latitude lines go across a map like the steps of a ladder.

When Father Marquette traveled on the Mississippi, he kept a journal. Each day he studied the sun and stars. They helped tell him the latitude of his position. He wrote the latitude in his journal. Later, this information could be used to make maps.

The lines which go up and down (north and south) are called **longitude** (LON ji tude). Longitude lines connect the North and South Poles.

Find Michigan on a globe. Follow the nearest latitude line. Most of the other places along that line will have a **climate** like Michigan's. Why would that be true? Because they all get about the same amount of sunlight.

The line on a globe at the fattest part of the earth is called the **equator**. This imaginary line goes around the middle of the earth. It is an *equal* distance from the North Pole and the South Pole. The land along the equator is the hottest.

Latitude lines north of the equator are named "north" latitude. Those south of the equator are "south" latitude. Of course, Michigan is north of the equator. All latitude lines crossing Michigan are north latitude lines.

The country of Britain is the starting point for longitude lines. One line at that place is labeled zero degrees (0°). Longitude lines west of Britain, like those in Michigan, are west longitude.

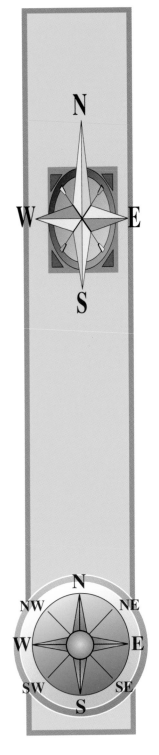

Where On Earth Are We?

Where exactly is Michigan? Can you find it on a map or globe? An easy way is to look for the Great Lakes. They surround Michigan. But, let's be more precise.

85°W

45°N

Michigan is about half-way between the North Pole and the equator. Did you know that? The halfway line crosses Michigan in the northern part of the Lower Peninsula. There is a sign along the highway near Gaylord. That sign shows the halfway point.

The line 45° north latitude crosses Michigan's Lower Peninsula. Art by Aaron Zenz.

Look at a Michigan map which shows where the halfway line crosses. Now find the tiny Mission Peninsula. This little finger of land is in Grand Traverse Bay. The halfway line almost touches the tip of the Mission Peninsula. Anytime you see Michigan, you can mark where this line crosses the state.

Halfway to the North Pole!

This halfway line has a name. It is called **45 degrees north latitude.** It is exactly halfway between the equator (the middle of the earth) and the North Pole. You may also see the ° symbol used for degrees. Father Marquette and Jolliet crossed this line soon after starting to the Mississippi River.

Follow the line 45° north latitude east or west and find other places. Each place is halfway between the equator and the North Pole- just like Michigan.

More Map Lines!

Longitude lines also go through Michigan. The line 83 degrees west longitude, passes near Detroit.

Latitude and longitude lines together tell the location of any place on earth! For example, Ionia, Michigan is at 43° north latitude and 85°west longitude. These two lines cross at Ionia.

The degrees (°) can be broken into smaller parts called "minutes." The symbol for minutes is (').You may see minutes along with degrees in printed information.

Father Marquette always knew his latitude and longitude measurements might be wrong. He could have made a mistake. Today, people using computers, radios, and satellites, can know exactly where they are. This is called **global positioning**.

Using global positioning, a location is told in latitude and longitude numbers. This information can also be used to locate a home or building. If your parents buy a new home, latitude and longitude might be used to tell exactly where it is.

LATITUDE

LONGITUDE

Questions to think about

1. If you made a map of your town, which compass direction should be at the top?

2. Draw a map compass in the center of a sheet of paper. Then label the four main directions and the four in-between directions.

3. Draw the equator on a sheet of paper. Add some lines of latitude and longitude. Label your lines.

4. Find your town on a map. Is your town closer to the equator or the North Pole?

Brain Stretchers
Is a place at 50 degrees north latitude and 90 degrees west longitude in Michigan? (Use a good map to help you decide.)

Try to discover the latitude and longitude of your city or town. (Some encyclopedias have a list of the global position of cities throughout the world.)

Compare the latitude and longitude of Detroit with other places in the world. Detroit is at about 43 degrees north latitude and 83 degrees west longitude. Find some other cities or countries along the lines 43 degrees north latitude or 83 degrees west longitude.

Words In Action!
Use lines of latitude and longitude to help another classmate travel from one Michigan city to another. Write clear directions to do this.

Chapter 3 Lesson 4
Some Grand Plans

Robert La Salle (lah sal) was a Frenchman with big plans. His older brother became a priest and came to Canada. Robert soon moved to Canada too. At first Robert tried farming but wanted more excitement. He began to explore and learn Indian languages.

La Salle

Gather Many Furs

La Salle made a grand plan. He was going to trade furs in a big way. He planned to build forts and trading posts farther west than anyone else. He would collect the furs on a large ship and take them east.

In 1677 La Salle returned to France and spoke with the king. La Salle got permission to build forts along the Mississippi River. The king said okay, but LaSalle would have to pay for everything himself!

La Salle had little money. He needed people to help pay for his plans. They would be **investors**. The investors would let La Salle use some of their money. They would **invest** in his plan. In return, La Salle would pay them part of the profits. The investors were taking a risk. They hoped to get their money back and some more.

Henri de Tonty— A Friend!

La Salle sailed back to New France. On the ship he met a man from Italy. The new friend was **Henri de Tonty** (on RAY day TON tee). Both Henri and his brother eventually came to Michigan. Henri was the first Italian to come to Michigan.

A Ship On the Great Lakes!

La Salle planned to trade furs. He would trade along the Great Lakes and along the Mississippi River. He would build a fur trading empire!

La Salle was going to build a full-sized sailing ship! He went to a place above the **Niagara Falls**. The Falls are between Lake Ontario and Lake Erie. There is no way to sail a ship around the great waterfalls. Because of this, his ship was built on the other side. La Salle and his men built the ship in the wilderness. While working, they kept an eye out for unfriendly Indians.

After much difficulty, the ship was finished and named the *Griffon*. There was nothing like this ship on the Upper Great Lakes. It had room for 45 tons of cargo and carried five cannons for protection.

First Stop, Detroit

In August, 1679 the *Griffon* set sail heading west. After three or four days it reached a place the French called the **de troit** (day twah). This is a narrow spot in the Lakes between the Lower Peninsula and Canada. Now, Michigan's largest city is there.

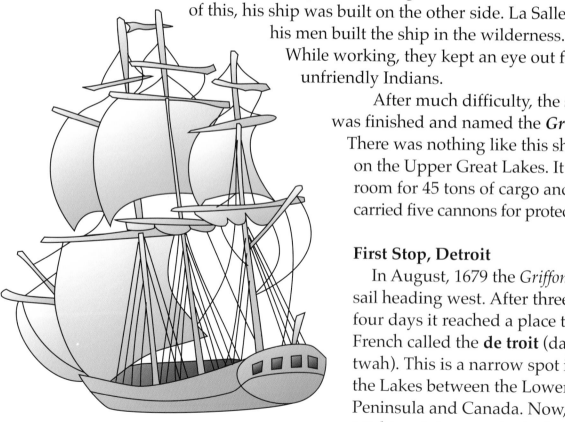

The first sailing ship above Niagara Falls was the *Griffon*. Art by Aaron Zenz.

The *Griffon* sailed on into Lake Huron and toward St. Ignace. When it arrived at St. Ignace, La Salle found a busy settlement. Many French traders had built homes there. There were also villages of Huron and Ottawa tribes. Crowds of Indians came to watch the *Griffon*. The Indians had never seen any ship like it.

Load the Furs

La Salle sent men ahead to trade for furs. The *Griffon* met the traders near Green Bay. It was time to send the furs back to Canada. They could be sold to help pay his investors. He sent the ship on and stayed behind.

Danger In the Air!

The furs were loaded on the *Griffon*. La Salle told the captain to sail quickly to Niagara, unload the furs, and return. The ship would meet La Salle at the southern end of Lake Michigan. He would wait near the St. Joseph River until it came back.

Before the ship left, some Indians told the captain a storm was coming. The captain was stubborn. He didn't see any sign of it, so he started anyway. Before the ship was out of sight, the storm came. The Griffon was tossed violently by the wind and waves! The storm lasted five days.

In 1680, LaSalle and his men had to walk across the Lower Peninsula. They were the first Europeans to see this part of Michigan. Art by Aaron Zenz.

A Long Wait

On November 1, 1679, La Salle's group paddled to the east side of Lake Michigan. Did the *Griffon* get through the storm? La Salle and his men waited all winter. Next spring his ship still did not come back. No one ever saw the Griffon again. It disappeared without a trace!

Through the Woods

La Salle's group had no choice. They would have to get back on their own. It was over 600 miles to **Montreal** (mon tree all). They must cross the entire Lower Peninsula and more!

In March they began to walk. There were no paths. The forests were full of thick bushes. No Europeans had gone this way before. La Salle said,

"...in two days and a half our clothes were all torn, and our faces so covered with blood that we hardly knew each other."

No Native Americans lived in the southern part of Michigan at that time. The land was claimed by five or six different tribes. The only ones who went there were warriors.

La Salle and his men walked all the way across Michigan. They were the first Europeans to see that part of our state. Finally they arrived at the Detroit River and crossed it on a raft. The men trudged on. La Salle asked about his ship at Niagara Falls and Montreal. No one had seen the *Griffon*. He had to face his investors and tell them he lost all their money! La Salle's grand plans turned into a grand disaster!

Cadillac— The Man Who Started Detroit

Soon another ambitious person came to Michigan. He was **Antoine Cadillac** (ahn TWAHN KAD el ak). Cadillac was another Frenchman who came to Canada.

Before coming to Michigan, Cadillac was a pirate. He attacked British ships. Britain and France often did not get along well. The French king was pleased with Cadillac. The king promised Cadillac command of a fort in New France.

Reward For A Good Job

Fort de Baude (day BODE) near St. Ignace was Cadillac's new fort. While there, he traded in furs. He shipped those furs back to his wife in Canada. Marie-Therese (ma REE TEH rez) was her name. She ran the fur business and sold the furs.

Madame Cadillac arrived at Detroit in October 1701. She was one of the first European women in Michigan. Art by Aaron Zenz.

Cadillac liked the extra money from trading furs. However, there was a problem. Fur traders from Britain started to visit Michigan too. The British had many settlements along the east coast of America. They sent traders west toward Michigan.

An Idea For A New Fort

Cadillac had an idea to keep British traders out of Michigan. He would build a new fort. He would locate it to control whose ships and canoes sailed past. Cadillac decided the narrow place between the Lower Peninsula and Canada would be a great spot.

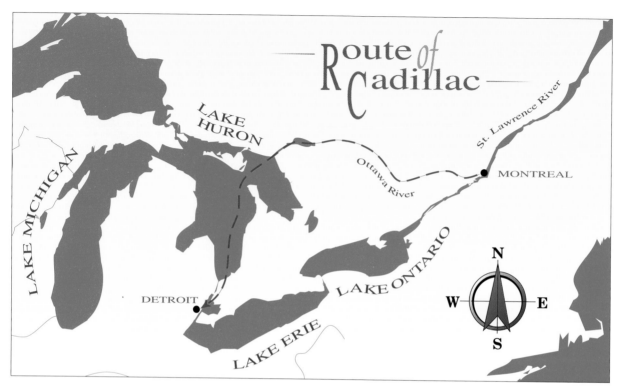

Today Detroit is the state's largest city. Art by Aaron Zenz.

Not Just A Fort

Cadillac's plan had some new ideas. He wanted to have many Indians move to Detroit. He also wanted French families to start farms there. Few French families lived in Michigan and there were hardly any farms.

Detroit Is Born!

On June 4, 1701, Cadillac left Montreal with 25 canoes. His second in command was Alphonse de Tonty. Alphonse (al FONs) was the brother of La Salle's friend, Henri de Tonty. By July 23rd, the group reached the Detroit River. The next day they started building. The French became the first Europeans to settle at Detroit. Now "Detroit" became the name of a town. It was more than just French words for a narrow place in the river.

The First French Women

Until now, no French women had come to Michigan. It was a rough land- a land of fur traders and explorers. Marie Cadillac and Anne de Tonty would come with their children. This excited the tribes. They felt it meant the French were here to stay. The French would be able to protect them when needed.

The ladies traveled in canoes with some of their children. Indians and soldiers did the paddling. It was a long and hard trip- almost 700 miles. When the women arrived, the men shouted and shot their guns in the air! It was October, 1701.

Success—But Problems Too

Yes, many Indians came to Detroit. The first winter there were 6,000 Indians living around the fort! The French began to **manufacture** products. There was a blacksmith, an armor maker, and a tool maker. The Cadillac family built three houses, two barns, a large windmill, and a bakery oven. Soon Detroit also had a church called Saint Anne's.

Cadillac had trouble though with the fur traders at Montreal. He was upsetting their business. By 1711, those traders decided to get him out of Detroit. They knew of a way to do it. They had the government give Cadillac a promotion. Cadillac was made governor of Louisiana.

CADILLAC'S FORT
AT DETROIT 1701

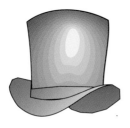

Beaver fur was used to make many kinds of hats. These hats did not look much like beaver fur when they were finished. The fur was first made into felt. It was the felt which was used for the hats.

Even though Cadillac left, Detroit kept going. Other French people came. Some of the early families still have relatives there today.

Let's Review

The French had been in Michigan for over 100 years. Still, not many French people had moved to Michigan. There were very few French farms or towns. Fur trading was still the only big business in Michigan.

Questions to think about

1. If you were a fur trader going back and forth to Mackinac Island in your canoe, would you like La Salle's plan? What might it do to your business?

2. Did the people who invested money in La Salle's plan make good profits? Explain.

3. Who began the city of Detroit?

4. What does the word Detroit mean?

5. When did the first European women reach Michigan? Name one of them.

Brain Stretchers

Someone once wrote, "Detroit was founded because an ancient King of France wore a beaver hat." Explain what this statement means.

Words In Action!

Imagine your job is to write an ad telling people about the chance to invest with La Salle. Write your ad and be sure to tell all of the risks. You want people to understand what they are doing with their money. You can put pictures in your ad too.

Chapter 3 Lesson 5
Trouble Between
the British and French

By 1751, the French had built seven forts in Michigan. These forts were built to protect their land. This land was a part of New France. The forts protected them from the tribes just in case a fight started. However, the French were more worried about another enemy. This enemy had many guns and cannons too. They were worried about the British!

The British had started many towns and farms. They had several times more people than the French. The French and British had done things differently. The French did not need too many people to trade furs. New France was a large land with few French people. So in 1754, the British decided to push the French out of North America. This became the **French and Indian War**.

The French and many Indians fought together against the British.

The British Want New France

Why did the British want New France? First of all, they did not like the French. The British knew they had more people and soldiers. They felt they could defeat the French in a war. Having New France would give them a larger fur trade and more land.

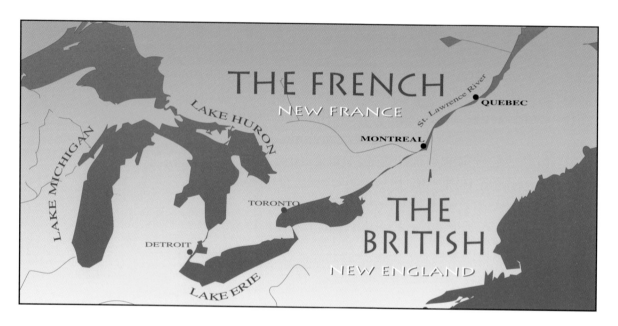

Quebec (KAY bek) was a main French fort. Quebec is on the St. Lawrence River in Canada. This key fort controlled who used the river. Ships could not pass by the fort's cannons. The French must not lose Quebec. If the French could not use the St. Lawrence, they would be in trouble. They could not send men and supplies to places like Michigan.

Warriors from some Michigan tribes had gone to Quebec. The tribes wanted to help the French win. Quebec's fort was on a large hill high above the river. For

a long time the British could not damage the fort. Then one night they discovered a way to sneak up the hill. The next morning there was a great battle. The French lost at Quebec! Soon the war ended and the British won. Now they controlled much of North America!

Why You Don't You Speak French

If the French had won, the language you speak might be French! Canada would belong to France too! Actually some people in Canada do speak French. They also have French customs. Canada has two languages, English and French.

What the French Left Behind

The French left some things behind for us. These are the names they used in Michigan. Our largest city, Detroit, has a French name. Other cities have French names too. Traverse City, St. Joseph, Marquette, and **Charlevoix** (SHAR la voy) are four examples. Some of our rivers also have French names. The Marquette and Au Sable are two long rivers with French names.

Major Gladwin was a British commander at Detroit in 1763. Courtesy of Michigan State Archives.

A New Flag In Michigan

In 1760, British soldiers marched into Detroit. Now Michigan "belonged" to Britain. It was a part of their **colonies** (KOL eh neez) in North America. Of course, they did not bother to ask the tribes if this was all right.

When the French left, it worried the tribes. They needed to trade for rifles, gunpowder, blankets, and more. The British did not see the tribes as friends. After all, the tribes had been fighting them. After a while, they traded a little. The British prices were high. The British would not trade for guns. The tribes were quite upset.

Chief Pontiac's War

An Ottawa chief named **Pontiac** (PON tee ak) thought about what to do. He lived across the river from Detroit. Pontiac had helped the French at Quebec. If the tribes could beat the British, would the French come back?

Pontiac invited many tribes to come to a meeting near Detroit. It was April 27, 1763. Chief Pontiac had a plan. He would ask to meet with the British in the fort. Pontiac would bring many warriors with him. Each man would be wearing a large blanket.

Danger at Detroit

Pontiac's warriors cut the barrels of their rifles short. The guns would be under their blankets when they walked into the fort! More Indians would be outside ready to run in and join the fight.

Pontiac's discouraged warriors leave the fort at Detroit. Major Gladwin discovered their plan to attack the British. Original art by Frederic Remington.

One morning 11 chiefs and 60 warriors solemnly walked into the fort. However, they soon realized something was wrong. The soldiers were not going about business as usual. They were armed and ready. Somehow the British learned of the plan!

During the meeting Pontiac talked briefly and then asked to leave. The British let the Indians go. Maybe they hoped Pontiac had changed his mind. The 120 or so British inside the fort knew they were in real danger. Pontiac had about 800 warriors outside!

Pontiac's War Begins- The Attack!

One day, yells and war cries came from the woods. Indians rushed up and tried to chop a hole in the wall with their **tomahawks**! (TOM ah hawks) Many Indians died trying to get into the fort at Detroit.

That night the Indians started fires against the wooden walls. British soldiers raced back and forth with buckets of water.

The battle for Detroit went on for days. The British were becoming desperate. They did not have many bullets or much food left.

All summer passed with the British closed up inside the fort at Detroit. Time was also against the Indians. It was now fall. They needed to go hunting and gather food for the winter. Warriors began to drift away with their families.

Longest in Our History

Near the end of October, Pontiac received a letter from the French. It told him France and Britain had made peace. The French would not come back. Pontiac called off the attack. It had lasted 153 days. It was the longest Indian battle in American history. The long battle showed Pontiac's skill as an organizer and warrior.

War Spread Far and Wide

The British had many worries in the summer of 1763. For one thing, Detroit was not the only fort the Indians had attacked. Many tribes worked together. Pontiac had sent messengers urging them to fight. The British lost five forts! Only Fort Detroit and two others held out. Then there was tragic news about **Fort Michilimackinac** (MISH ill eh MACK in aw) at Mackinaw City.

Secret Plans For Michilimackinac

One day many Indians came into the fort to trade. Some British were puzzled. The only thing the Indians wanted were tomahawks! One trader, Alexander Henry, wrote something like this in his diary.

*A Chipeway came to tell me that his nation was going to play at **bag gat i way** with another Indian nation for a large bet. He invited me to witness the sport. He said the commandant was to be there, and would bet on the side of the Chipeways. I went to the commandant and talked with him a little. I wondered if the Indians might possibly have something evil in mind. The commandant only smiled at my suspicions.*

The Big Game

Many of the soldiers came out to watch the game. It was a great sight! The British commander made his bet on the Ojibwa side. It was a warm day, but the Indian women sat wrapped in blankets near the gate. Suddenly the ball went over the wall and into the fort.

The players rushed in after it. As they ran, they grabbed weapons from under the women's blankets. Few of the soldiers had time to defend themselves. It was a quick victory for the tribes. Many soldiers were killed, but Alexander Henry lived.

The Fighting Is Finished

This was part of the greatest American Indian war. It was called Pontiac's War. Not until 1766 did Pontiac and other chiefs smoke a peace pipe with the British. Pontiac showed great courage. He was a leader trying to keep his people's land.

The British government worried about more trouble with the Indians. The tribes were angry because settlers were taking their land. So, the British passed a law stopping settlers. The law said no settlers could go west of the Appalachian Mountains. They hoped that would keep the tribes happy.

For now, Michigan would remain a land of tribes, fur traders, and only a few settlers. British soldiers stayed at Fort Detroit and Fort Michilimackinac to keep the peace.

The Appalachian Mountains made it hard for pioneers to travel west. There were only a few good places to cross them. Map by Aaron Zenz.

77

Jean de Sable.
Art by Aaron Zenz.

The Black Trader

In the mid-1760s an unusual explorer and trader came to Michigan. His name was **Jean de Sable** (jHAN day SAW bul). De Sable was a black man with a French background. He was born in Haiti, an island southeast of Florida.

Jean was sent to school in France, but later moved to New Orleans. New Orleans is on the mouth of the Mississippi River. Then the Spanish took over that city. De Sable decided to move north. Finally, he arrived in Michigan.

It is said de Sable became good friends with Chief Pontiac. Jean lived near his camp, trading with the tribes. When Pontiac left Michigan, so did de Sable. In 1779, de Sable settled along the southern shore of Lake Michigan. Years later his settlement became a huge city. Today we call it Chicago.

Later, the British went to Chicago and took de Sable prisoner. They believed he was working against them. Jean de Sable was kept at Mackinaw for some time. Finally, he was allowed to go to Port Huron. Here he became a trader until the mid-1780s.

Jean de Sable died in 1818 at St. Charles, Missouri. Jean de Sable was probably the first African American in Michigan.

Questions to think about

1. Why isn't Michigan still a part of New France?

2. Why did Chief Pontiac want to attack the British forts?

3. Was the British commander at Fort Michilimackinac very smart?

4. Is this true or false? "After Pontiac's War, the British gave each family a free cabin if they moved to Michigan." Explain your answer.

5. Tell something interesting about Jean de Sable.

Brain Stretchers:
How far is it from Quebec to Detroit. Name two other cities which are about the same distance from Detroit.

Words In Action!
Imagine you are Chief Pontiac. You have decided to write a letter to the King of Britain. You want to explain why the British should treat the tribes better.

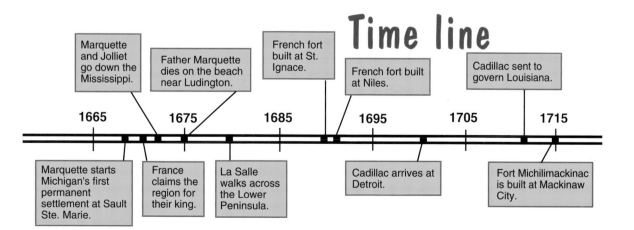

Time line

Marquette and Jolliet go down the Mississippi.

Father Marquette dies on the beach near Ludington.

French fort built at St. Ignace.

French fort built at Niles.

Cadillac sent to govern Louisiana.

1665   1675   1685   1695   1705   1715

Marquette starts Michigan's first permanent settlement at Sault Ste. Marie.

France claims the region for their king.

La Salle walks across the Lower Peninsula.

Cadillac arrives at Detroit.

Fort Michilimackinac is built at Mackinaw City.

Chapter 3 Lesson 6

Michigan and the Birth of the United States

By the late 1700s the British colonies in America wanted to be free. They did not like the British king telling them what to do. They did not like being told that they could not move west and settle. The people wanted to be Americans, not British. The colonies began a **revolution** in the spring of 1775 to start their own country. This was called the Revolutionary War or the War for Independence.

The British Cause Trouble

Michigan was far from the colonies, but British soldiers were here. **Kentucky** was the closest place with very many American settlers. British soldiers from Detroit attacked the Americans in Kentucky. The British urged Indians to go to Kentucky and attack settlers too.

The Indian attacks in Kentucky were very bad in 1777. The settlers called that time "the year of the bloody sevens." Many settlers were killed. Some were even kidnapped and brought to Detroit. The great **Daniel Boone (BOON)** was even one of

George Rogers Clark was a part of the War for Independence in the late 1700s. He led a group of American soldiers against the British. They had to make a long march during the winter through swamps and wetlands. Art by Aaron Zenz.

those. Daniel Boone was a famous pioneer and explorer. The Indians were very proud of catching him.

Americans Take Action

These attacks must be stopped! A young American soldier named **George Rogers Clark** headed west with 127 men. The group marched all the way from **Virginia**. The American soldiers captured a British fort in Ohio and one in Indiana. The Americans now blocked the way from Detroit to Kentucky. Clark and his soldiers were heroes!

George Rogers Clark planned to capture Detroit too. That did not happen. There was a shortage of supplies. The American soldiers stayed in Ohio instead.

Daniel Boone was captured by Indians in Kentucky. They brought him to Detroit to show him off. Art by Aaron Zenz

The British kept Detroit, but they lost much of their power in the area. Clark and his soldiers had done an important job. Their work helped to make Michigan a part of the United States.

The War for Independence lasted until 1783. Then the colonies were free! Each colony became a state in the new United States of America.

The British Are Sore Losers!

But wait! The British did not leave Michigan! They stayed in their forts. They traded for furs with the tribes.

General Wayne. Wayne county is named after him. Courtesy Michigan State Archives.

They gave guns to some tribes so they could attack more American settlers. This was not fair! Michigan did not belong to the British any longer!

The Americans became fed up. Finally President Washington sent **General Anthony Wayne** west with many soldiers. It was his job to kick out the British. He also had to control the tribes who caused trouble. In 1794, there was a huge battle near Toledo, Ohio. General Wayne defeated the British and Indians there. The tribes made peace **treaties** with the United States.

Michigan Joins the U.S.

Two years later the British left Michigan. In 1796, Michigan was really a part of the United States. The forts at Detroit and Mackinac Island were now filled with American soldiers. They stayed on alert because the British were not far away. Canada still belonged to the British. The enemy was just across the water!

General Wayne Leaves His Name Behind

General Wayne kept his headquarters in Detroit for about four years. Then he left to go back home. Sadly, he died on the trip.

People were proud of General Wayne and what his soldiers had done. Wayne County is named after the general. Today that county has more people than any other in Michigan.

A New Era, A New Chapter

The French had been here for 140 years. The British were in charge from 1760 to 1796- only 36 years. How long has Michigan been a part of the United States?

When the United States took over Michigan, big changes began. For a long time, Michigan had been a land of Indian tribes and European soldiers. Michigan had few settlers and few farms or towns. Soon all of these things would change. Michigan would start to grow in a hurry.

Questions To Think About

1. Whose soldiers were in Michigan during the War for Independence?

2. What did the soldiers in Detroit do to make life hard for the American settlers?

3. Which American soldier thought about attacking Detroit during the War for Independence?

4. Who forced the British to finally leave Michigan?

Brain Stretchers
Make a chart to compare how long each country- France, Britain, and the United States- has ruled Michigan.

Words In Action!
Imagine you lived in Detroit during the War for Independence. Write a letter to a friend telling about what is happening. You might mention the tribes bringing kidnapped people like Daniel Boone. You might tell if people were worried about an American attack.

Chapter 4   Lesson 1

Becoming A State-
It Was Not Easy!

What were the biggest changes pioneers made to Michigan?
What was the most important part of starting a new state?

Three Strikes Against the British

So far the United States fought with Britain twice. The first time was the War for Independence. General Wayne fought them a second time a few years later. Now more trouble was brewing.

You should know what Michigan was like in those days. Michigan was a land of thick forests and Indian villages. Fur trading was still Michigan's biggest business. Many people here spoke French. Detroit was the only place like a city. Michigan had a large fort at Detroit and another on Mackinac Island. The British had a fort right across the Detroit River. There were hardly any roads. Most people and supplies reached Michigan by ship.

Michigan was not yet a state. It was just a **territory**. Its capital was Detroit. People could not vote on laws or have elections in a territory. The President of the United States appointed most of the officials. He named **William Hull** to be governor.

Governor
William Hull

The War of 1812

Some important battles in the War of 1812 were fought in and near Michigan. The American soldiers lost at Monroe and gave up Detroit. They won on Lake Erie and the Battle of the Thames (timz) in Canada.

We Have Had Enough! The War of 1812

The British had been a thorn in the side of our young country. They bothered us in several ways. The British had been stopping our ships on the ocean. They still encouraged Native Americans to attack our settlers. Finally the United States became angry and declared war. Our country was not prepared. The war did not go well for our side.

First, the British made a sneak attack on Fort Mackinac and captured it!

Governor Hull was made a general. He and his soldiers crossed the river to attack **Fort Malden**, the British Fort.

Then General Hull began to worry about the Indians. Many of them fought on the British side. Hull was afraid Indians would attack Detroit. The general decided to go back to the city.

Judge Woodward had just jumped out of bed when a British cannon-ball blasted through it! Art by Aaron Zenz.'

War of 1812

Oh, No!

The next thing people in Detroit knew, British cannon balls were falling on their homes! One family was just starting to eat breakfast. A cannon ball fell through the roof. It smashed through the table and went into the basement. It did not hurt them, but they left in a hurry! Another man had just gotten out of bed to see what was happening. Then a cannon ball blasted his bed to pieces.

The British soldiers and Indians crossed the river. They marched toward Detroit. General Hull had his cannon ready to fire. His soldiers were tense, but prepared to put up a good fight. Then General Hull did a surprising thing. He told his men to surrender. He did not ask anyone. The men and women could not believe it. The British soldiers walked in and took Detroit without a shot being fired.

People have always wondered if General Hull did the right thing. His action saved lives though. Detroit was one of the few American cities ever captured by another country.

The Biggest Battle

The Americans were not going to give up so easily. Other American soldiers came from the south to take back Detroit. The British attacked them at **Monroe** near the River Raisin. Over two thousand men were in the fight. This was the biggest battle ever fought in Michigan. The Americans had to surrender this time. We were beaten.

Who Will Control the Lakes?

In this war the British also had ships on Lake Erie. These ships brought supplies to their soldiers. **Oliver Hazard Perry** was a young officer in the American navy. He had been building ships to fight the British. Finally, the British ships and Perry's ships went to battle. There were six British ships and nine American ships. The fight was fierce. Bullets and cannon balls whizzed through the air.

Our American ships were not doing well. Most of the sailors on Perry's ship had been killed or wounded. The British thought they had won, but Perry would not give up. There was one American ship with only a little damage. Perry risked his life to reach it. He got into a rowboat and left his ship. Perry took charge of the undamaged warship. Then he sailed into the British and began firing. Amazingly, the Americans finally won.

Lieutenant Oliver Hazard Perry left his damaged ship and rowed to another. He and his men won the battle against the British on Lake Erie.

Now the Americans controlled Lake Erie! The British were in trouble, because they could not get supplies. All the newspapers in the country told of the victory!

Another Point of View

Let's look at the war from another point of view. Many Native Americans fought with the British. One of them was called **Tecumseh**.

Tecumseh lived in a time of great trouble for his people. The tribes did not want American settlers on their land.

Tecumseh Speaks!

One time Tecumseh heard of a new treaty between a tribe and the United States government. He became very upset. In his own language he said, "Sell a country! Why not sell the air, the clouds, and the great sea, as well as the earth? Did not the Great Spirit make them all for the use of his children?" He felt the land belonged to all tribes, not just the one which signed the treaty.

When the War of 1812 started, Tecumseh joined the British side. The British were eager for help. The Americans greatly feared Tecumseh and the other Native American warriors.

Tecumseh, a strong and proud Indian leader, fought with the British in the War of 1812. Here he is wearing part of a British uniform. Art by Aaron Zenz.

The British Pull Out

Once the Americans controlled Lake Erie, the British wanted to leave Fort Malden. When Tecumseh heard about this, he gave an angry speech. He told the British commanders they were cowards. When he finished talking, all the Indians jumped up and shook their tomahawks!

The British left and Tecumseh followed. They retreated across Canada. Finally the Americans caught the British and Indians. There was a terrible battle. Tecumseh was killed and the British defeated in 1813.

Finally the two governments made peace in 1814. The war was over! The British left Detroit and Michigan for good. We did keep our forts- just in case!

Questions to think about

1. What country did we fight in the War of 1812?

2. In the War of 1812 two important places in Michigan were captured. One was Fort Mackinac. What was the other place?

3. Why was Perry's victory on Lake Erie important? After the battle what did we control? What was the main way of moving supplies at that time?

4. Why did Tecumseh and other Native Americans fight in the War of 1812?

5. There was a very big battle in Michigan during the War of 1812. What city was this battle near?

Brain Stretchers
The Great Lakes and the St. Lawrence River are part of an important waterway. This waterway connects our region to the Atlantic Ocean. During wars different sides wanted to control it. Explain why.

Words In Action!
The army put General Hull on trial because he surrendered Detroit. Imagine you are one of the lawyers. Write an argument for or against General Hull.

Chapter 4 Lesson 2

Pioneers, On The Way!

People Needed Land

Michigan was a very different place in the early 1800s. At that time most people earned a living by farming. Land was becoming scarce in the eastern states. It was quite expensive to buy enough land to start a new farm. Younger families started to move west.

Cheap Land In Michigan!

Land was cheap in Michigan. It cost a dollar or two an **acre.** What does an acre of land cost today?

Reaching Michigan was another matter. The traveling was hard. The roads were very bad, if there were any at all. A wagon might only travel a dozen miles a day.

A pioneer cabin -- from the inside and the outside. Top picture courtesy of the Michigan State Archives.

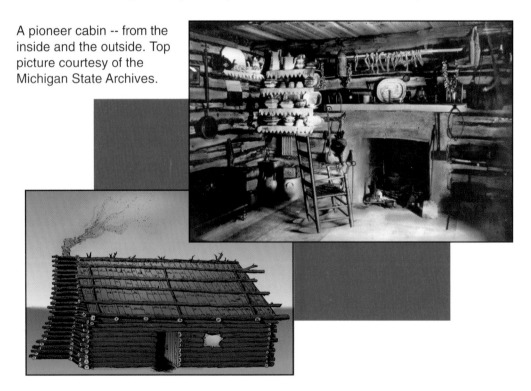

Almost everyone moving west, came through Ohio. Some pioneers stayed there. So, Ohio became a state over 30 years before Michigan.

New Ways to Reach Michigan

In the 1820s and 1830s new ways to travel took shape. Now, some ships were powered by steam engines. They could travel even when the wind did not blow. People were also building **canals**.

Today, we do not talk much about canals, but they were very useful at one time. Canals are man-made rivers. Horses pulled small shallow boats along the canal. Now people could travel to places that had no rivers.

Pioneers & the Erie Canal

one day's travel on the canal
one day's travel by wagon

The Erie Canal opened the route to Michigan and thousands of families traveled down it. Map by Aaron Zenz.

The **Erie Canal** was one of the most important canals. It went to Lake Erie from the Hudson River in New York state. Now people went from New York City to Detroit by boat.

Many of the new settlers came from the state of New York. Almost all of them headed to Detroit. The area around Detroit began to grow quickly.

Using the canal, it was much easier to reach the cheap land in Michigan! Our population grew and grew. In 1820 we only had 8,765 people; by 1840 we had 212,267!

William Nowlin was a pioneer boy. He came to Michigan with his family in 1834. This is what he has to say.......

On the Way to Michigan! (1834)

Let me introduce myself. I am William Nowlin. I was born in the state of New York. I was 11 years of age, when the word Michigan first grated upon my ear. Father talked continually of Michigan, though Mother was very much opposed to leaving her home.

I am the oldest of five children. I was very much opposed to coming to Michigan too. I did all that a boy of my age could do to prevent it. The thought of Indians, bears, and wolves terrified me.

My mother's health was very poor. Many of her friends said she would not live to get to Michigan. She thought she could not survive the journey. She said that if she did, herself and family would be killed by the Indians, perish in the wilderness, or starve to death.

We did leave, however, early in the spring of 1834. Our friends were weeping for they thought we were going "out of the world."

We traveled about fifty miles which brought us to Utica, New York. There we boarded a canal boat and moved slowly night and day, to invade the forests of Michigan.

When it was pleasant, we spent part of the time on the top of the long, low cabin. One day mother left my little brother, then four years old, in the care of my oldest sister, Rachel. Little brother decided to have a rock in an easy chair, rocked over, and took a cold bath in the canal.

Mother and I were in the cabin when we heard the cry, "Overboard"! We rushed on deck, and the first thing we saw was a man swimming with something ahead of him. It proved to be my brother held by the strong arm of an English gentleman. That Englishman was our ideal hero for many years. His bravery and skill was unparalleled by anything we had seen. He had saved our brother from a watery grave. That brother is now the John Smith Nowlin of Dearborn.

When we arrived at Buffalo, the steamer "Michigan", was just ready for her second trip. We started the next morning.

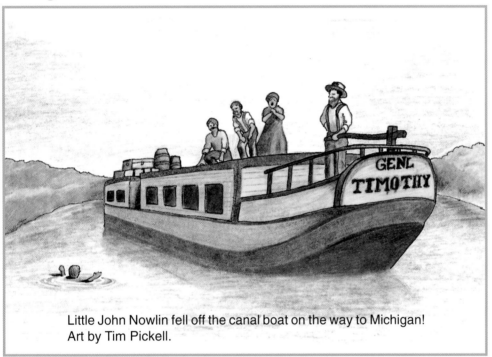

Little John Nowlin fell off the canal boat on the way to Michigan!
Art by Tim Pickell.

There was a great storm on the way across Lake Erie. People thought the ship was finished, but we arrived safely at Detroit. Mother did not die. No one was killed by Indians. Father bought some land near Dearborn and started a farm. It has been hard work but we made it!

Settlers like the Nowlins bought their land from the government. The government got the land from the tribes. This is how that happened.....

Getting the Land

The United States government made **treaties** with the tribes to give up their land. The government paid the tribes, but it was not that much. Some tribes kept the right to hunt and fish. At least they should be able to feed themselves.

Sometimes a tribe did not really want to make a treaty. They did not want trouble with the army, so they gave in. Between 1795 and 1842 the tribes gave up nearly all of Michigan.

LAND TREATIES WITH MICHIGAN TRIBES

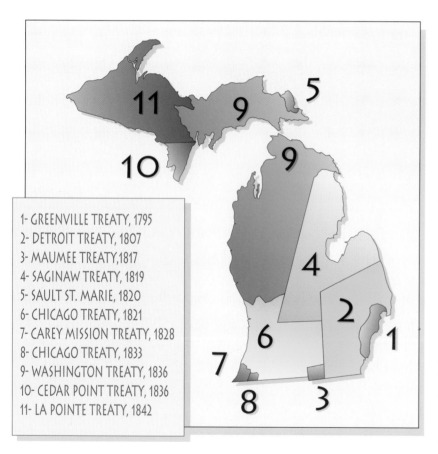

1- GREENVILLE TREATY, 1795
2- DETROIT TREATY, 1807
3- MAUMEE TREATY, 1817
4- SAGINAW TREATY, 1819
5- SAULT ST. MARIE, 1820
6- CHICAGO TREATY, 1821
7- CAREY MISSION TREATY, 1828
8- CHICAGO TREATY, 1833
9- WASHINGTON TREATY, 1836
10- CEDAR POINT TREATY, 1836
11- LA POINTE TREATY, 1842

The Story of a Treaty

Here is the story of a treaty and the Ojibwa woman who helped with it. Daughter of the Green Mountain was born near the year 1776. We do not know the exact time. When she was a young woman, she met a fur trader. His name was John Johnston.

In 1793 they were married. Daughter of the Green Mountain was then known as Susan Johnston.

The Johnstons had a trading post at Sault Ste. Marie. They were leaders in the town. Visitors always had a warm greeting in their home.

In 1820 a man named **Lewis Cass** and a small group of soldiers came to Sault Ste. Marie. They came to make a treaty with the tribes. Mr. Cass wanted the land around the Soo for the United States.

Mr. Cass met with a large, angry group of Indians. They did not want a treaty! One of the chiefs ran over to a flag pole and raised the British flag. This action upset Lewis Cass and he yanked down the flag. Susan Johnston was afraid the Indians would kill Mr. Cass and his small group.

She spoke to the tribal leaders. She carefully explained what would happen if they killed Lewis Cass and the Americans. She said many soldiers would come and punish them. Many Indians would die. She was able to get the Ojibwa leaders to sign a treaty. Susan said that peace was more important in the long run.

Lewis Cass said the United States was grateful. He was glad Susan Johnston helped him.

Susan Johnston's talk with the Ojibwa chiefs saved Lewis Cass and his men. Art by Aaron Zenz.

Mapping the Land

Before the land could be sold to settlers, there had to be a system to know exactly where each property was located. This was not simple with woods and forests everywhere.

The government hired **surveyors** to go and look over the land. The surveyors traveled over the hills and through swamps. The surveyors used maps, compasses and links of chain to measure the land. It was hard work.

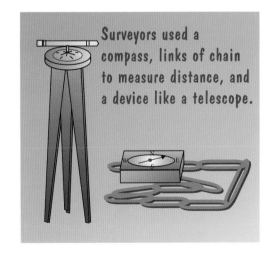

Surveyors used a compass, links of chain to measure distance, and a device like a telescope.

95

Pigs were easy to keep and feed by Michigan's first farmers. The pigs also killed rattlesnakes which were found in the swamps.

Buying the Land

Each settler looked for some good land where no one else lived. Then he or she went to a **land office**. Using the surveyors' information and maps, the settler described the land. The price set for most land was $1.25 an acre. The money was paid and a **deed** given to the settler. A deed is an official proof of ownership.

New Ways Are So Different

This way of owning land seemed very strange to the tribes. The way the land was to be used was very different too. The Native Americans moved from place to place hunting and trapping. Now farmers were going to cut down the trees and plant crops. Roads and towns would be built. It would be almost impossible for the two cultures to live together.

Too Many Trees

It is hard to realize how many trees were here then. They covered almost the whole state. Trees wouldn't let enough light reach the crops. The farmer's corn or wheat could not grow. If the trees stayed, the farmer could not. Thousands and thousands of trees were cut down.

Next, they plowed the ground. There were no tractors. A team of oxen was often used. The farmer had to walk behind the plow and guide it. There were many tree stumps and large rocks to move.

A pioneer's table might have looked like this at dinner time.

Pioneer farmers had to make or grow almost every-thing they needed. There might not be a store or town for miles- and traveling was difficult.

Questions to think about

1. Why did the pioneers want to come to Michigan?

2. Why didn't more settlers come until the 1830s?

3. What important improvements in travel helped early settlers reach Michigan?

4. Where is the Erie Canal?

5. What did Susan Johnston do?

6. List all the ways the pioneers changed Michigan.

Brain Stretchers
Find out which treaty was made for the land which includes your town. The map on page 94 can help you. Use the internet to find out what this treaty said.

Imagine coming to Detroit from Albany, New York long ago. Compare how long it took using the Erie Canal and how long it took to come by wagon. Use a graph to show your results.

Words In Action!
Core democratic values (kor dim oh kra tik val youz) are the main ideas for our kind of government. Go to page 251 for a list of these values. Decide if any of them were not followed well when the treaties were made with Michigan's tribes. Explain your answer.

Chapter 4 Lesson 3

Laws and People in the Young Land

Just a Wilderness in the Northwest

Soon after the War for Independence, Michigan was made a part of the **Northwest Territory**. This was in 1787. The Northwest Territory was a very large area. Later, it was divided into several states. Ohio, Illinois, Indiana, Michigan, and Wisconsin were all in this first big territory.

Why did they use the name Northwest Territory? At that time the United States was much smaller. This land was in the northwest corner- that is why!

An Important Set of Laws

In 1787 the national government passed a law about the Northwest Territory. It is called the Northwest **Ordinance.** This law told some basic rules about life in the territory. Here is what it said about growing from a territory into a state.

Step 1.
In the beginning a territory has no elected officials. It is governed by a governor and three judges. The President of the United States names these people.

Step 2.
Once there are 5,000 free adult men, an elected **legislature** is formed. The governor approves all laws. The governor and judges are still named by the President.

Step 3.
Once there are 60,000 people in the territory, it can become a state. It will be equal to all the other states.

Who Has the Power?

When you read these parts of the law, who do you see having the power? It does not mention women. It says free adult men. Did you know women could not even vote for over 130 years more! This also means slaves did not count. The President says who is in charge. The President might not be in touch with happenings in the wilderness. The wrong sort of people might be put in charge. This is one reason people wanted to become a state as soon as possible. They wanted to have their own say.

Some Key Points

This does not mean the ordinance was a bad law. The Northwest Ordinance had some good points. Many basic things about Michigan first came from that set of laws. Here are some other things the Northwest Ordinance said:

1.   Slavery was to be stopped in this area. (*People who already owned slaves were allowed to keep them.*)

2.   Indians were to be treated with fairness. No land would be taken from them without their agreement.

3.   Schools and education would always be encouraged because "religion, morality and knowledge are necessary to good government and the happiness of mankind."

You know the tribes did not get a wonderful deal with their land. There were people in those times , however, who felt they should not get anything. There were those who thought of them as only a beaten enemy.

Over the years, states were made out of the Northwest Territory. The boundaries changed several times. The national government formed the Michigan Territory in 1805. At times the Michigan Territory had more land than our state does now.

During the 18 years Lewis Cass was governor of the Michigan Territory he did many things. He wrote the state motto and designed the state seal. He made treaties with the tribes. He explored the land.

Who Was Lewis Cass?

When Michigan was a territory, Lewis Cass was the governor for many years. Remember he was not elected by people in Michigan. He was given the job by the President. Even so, Lewis did a good job. He worked hard to help Michigan grow.

Lewis Cass was born in New Hampshire in 1782. As a young man he moved with his family to Ohio.

Lewis Cass became a soldier and fought in the War of 1812. He was one of the soldiers at Detroit when General Hull surrendered it to the British.

In 1813 he became governor of the Michigan Territory. He kept this job for eighteen years.

Lewis Cass left his mark on Michigan history. He suggested the state motto. He designed the state seal. Cass City and Cassopolis were named for him. A county and a river also have his name.

A Young New Leader

While Cass was governor of the territory, John Mason was named secretary. Mason brought his 18-year-old son

to the office with him. His son's name was Stevens T. Mason. He often helped his father with the work. His father took care of the governor's duties when Cass was away.

The older Mr. Mason thought his job was boring. He wanted to go to Texas. Before heading for Texas, Lewis Cass and the Masons went to meet President Jackson. Mr. Mason asked the President if his son could take over his job. President Jackson really liked the young man and agreed. That was how Stevens T. Mason became secretary for the Michigan Territory when he was only 19. He was not even old enough to vote!

Then Stevens T. Mason got a surprise. He found out Lewis Cass would be gone too. Cass was to become the U.S. Secretary of War. Cass would stay in Washington D.C.

Stevens T. Mason was given the nickname of "Boy Governor"

The Boy Is In Charge?

When Stevens T. Mason came back to Detroit, many people were upset. How could the President appoint such a youngster? A crowd of 2,000 gathered in Detroit to speak out against him. I wonder if he was scared?

Stevens told everyone he would always be ready to listen to the advice of older people. He was able to convince the crowd. Still he was given the nickname "Boy Governor."

Later, President Jackson did send another governor. This man was often away. Once when he happened to be in town, **cholera** struck and he died. The President did not name another governor.

Hey, We Are Ready!

Ohio, Illinois, and Indiana became states, but Michigan was still a territory. By 1834, we had more than enough people living here to become a state. Stevens T. Mason asked the **Congress** in **Washington, D.C.,** to vote and let Michigan become a state. Congress said, "Not so fast."

What was the problem? Didn't Congress want new states? Well, we had been arguing with Ohio over the little village where Toledo is today. The boundary lines showed it to be in Michigan, but Ohio thought it was theirs.

Territory of Michigan

Jonesville

Hillsdale

Adrian

Monroe

Lake Erie

line claimed by Ohio

line claimed by Michigan   Toledo

State of Ohio   ← *Maumee River*

Based on the S. Augustus Mitchell map of 1834

In the 1830s Michigan and Ohio argued over the border between them. The people of Michigan felt Toledo should be in Michigan. This strip of land in southern Michigan was called the Toledo Strip.

War With Ohio? You Must Be Kidding!

When neighbors argue about property lines, they often become upset easily. The same thing happened between Michigan and Ohio. Everyone thought Toledo would become an important city.

Michigan men chased surveyors from Ohio away from the Toledo Strip. Some people called the argument the "Toledo War."

Chapter 4 *Becoming a State-- It Was Not Easy!*

Michigan sent soldiers to Toledo to keep it for Michigan. There were a few fights. A few people who were for Ohio were kidnapped. No one was killed though. This argument with Ohio was known as the **Toledo War**.

A Trade!

President Jackson said this foolishness must stop! It was finally suggested we give up the Toledo area for the western Upper Peninsula. This land had not been a part of Michigan.

Some Michiganians did not think this was a good idea. They thought the Upper Peninsula was too far away and was a frozen wasteland. Was it good for anything? Well, it had trees for lumber and copper and iron too. It was a very good trade!

At last, Congress let us become a state in 1837. Stevens T. Mason was the first governor of the state of Michigan. That is the story of how we now have two peninsulas. It is also the story of how Toledo, Ohio might have been Toledo, Michigan.

How Michigan Grew...

As the number of pioneers went up, the number of Indians went down. A census is an official count of the people living in a place.

Year	People	(does not include Native Americans)
1773	1,550	more or less, British census of Detroit was 1,367 and included slaves
1810	5,000	more or less
1820	8,896	really slightly less- includes extra land
1830	31,639	really slightly less- includes extra land
1834	87,278	special census (1,422 lived in the U.P.)
1837	174,543	special census
1840	212,267	U.S census

Between 1830 and 1840 Michigan grew faster than any other state or territory!

People
People
People

Michigan's Capital

When we were a territory, the capital was in Detroit. Detroit stayed the capital until 1847. Then some people felt the capital should be nearer the middle of the state. When people heard about the idea, everyone wanted it in their town!

Then the legislature voted. They could not decide. No one wanted to vote for someone else's town. Finally, someone said make it Lansing. Lansing? Where is that? There were only a few cabins in Lansing then. The next time they voted everyone was shocked. Lansing won and the capital was moved.

Today, Lansing is a large city. The capital is still there. The capitol building you see now was built in 1879.

Some of Michigan's EARLY CITIES!

Marquette
-1849-

Sault Ste. Marie
-1668-

St. Ignace
-1671-

Menominee
-1836-

Saginaw
-1816-

Grand Rapids
-1820-

Flint
-1819-

Port Huron
-1790-

Lansing
-1835-

Pontiac
-1818-

Kalamazoo
-1829-

Detroit
-1701-

Dearborn
-1795-

Monroe
-1780-

Questions to think about

1. Who was Lewis Cass?

2. Who was Stevens T. Mason?

3. What problem kept Michigan from becoming a state for a while? When did it become a state?

4. What happened so all of the Upper Peninsula became a part of Michigan?

5. Write the rules the early settlers had to follow to become a state.

Brain Stretchers
Make a chart or graph showing how the population of Michigan grew.

Make a time line using as many of the dates in this chapter as you can. An example is shown below.

Words In Action!
Read the first two key points from the Northwest Ordinance on page 99. They deal with slavery and Michigan's Indians. Check the list of core democratic values on page 251. Write a paragraph explaining which ones go along with the key points 1 and 2 on page 99.

Time line

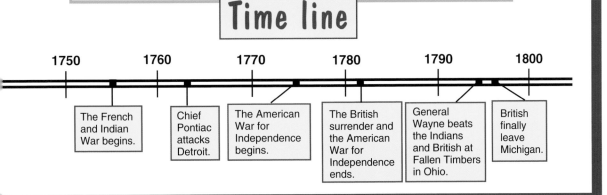

| 1750 | 1760 | 1770 | 1780 | 1790 | 1800 |

The French and Indian War begins.

Chief Pontiac attacks Detroit.

The American War for Independence begins.

The British surrender and the American War for Independence ends.

General Wayne beats the Indians and British at Fallen Timbers in Ohio.

British finally leave Michigan.

Chapter 5

Lesson 1

Slavery and the Trouble That Followed

How did slavery divide the country and lead to a war?

The United States has always been famous as the home of the free. At first we were not honest about this because we allowed **slavery**.

No Slaves Here- But....

The Northwest Ordinance said slavery would be stopped in Michigan. Still, there were a few slaves here. By the 1830s there were hardly any. Many people in Michigan knew slavery was very wrong. Sadly, people in other parts of the country felt slavery was all right. Most slaves were held in the southern states.

Some people tried to have slavery outlawed. It was not easy. Slaves were treated like useful property. They were treated like animals or pieces of equipment- like horses or plows.

Can't We Stop It?

During the 1830s, feelings against slavery increased. Many settlers in Michigan came from New York state. There had been little slavery in New York. So, most people here felt slavery should be ended.

In 1834 Canada made slavery illegal. Now it was against the law to own a slave in that country. From time to time slaves ran away. Before 1834 they had no place to go. Their owners could track them down wherever they went. Now, if a slave could only reach Canada, he or she was free. No one could come after them!

Michigan- the Way to Freedom

Since Michigan is right next to Canada, our state became one pathway to freedom. There were those who wanted to help runaway slaves. If they saw an escaped slave family, they let them rest in their barn and gave them a meal. Sometimes they built secret rooms in their homes as hiding places.

After a while the slave helpers became more organized. They talked with one another. They planned stops along the way. They figured out ways to take the slaves across the Detroit River and at other places.

Members of the Underground Railroad often hid escaped slaves in their homes and barns. Art by Aaron Zenz.

The Underground Railroad

These slave helpers developed into a secret group. The group was secret because it was against the law to help escaped slaves. They were called the **Underground Railroad**. This group had no real trains and it was not under the ground. Each hiding place was called a station. The helpers were called conductors. Slaves were moved, usually at night, from station to station in wagons.

Many towns in Michigan had Underground Railroad stations. Look at the map and see if you can find your town. Not all towns with stations are shown. Even if it is not on the map, it may have had a station.

This map shows many routes which were used by the Underground Railroad. Most led to Canada.

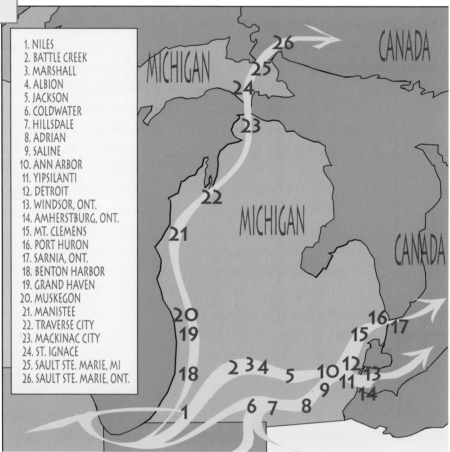

1. NILES
2. BATTLE CREEK
3. MARSHALL
4. ALBION
5. JACKSON
6. COLDWATER
7. HILLSDALE
8. ADRIAN
9. SALINE
10. ANN ARBOR
11. YIPSILANTI
12. DETROIT
13. WINDSOR, ONT.
14. AMHERSTBURG, ONT.
15. MT. CLEMENS
16. PORT HURON
17. SARNIA, ONT.
18. BENTON HARBOR
19. GRAND HAVEN
20. MUSKEGON
21. MANISTEE
22. TRAVERSE CITY
23. MACKINAC CITY
24. ST. IGNACE
25. SAULT STE. MARIE, MI
26. SAULT STE. MARIE, ONT.

Women Speak Out - Sojourner Truth

An ex-slave woman from New York moved to **Battle Creek** in 1850. She was a tall, proud woman. Others imagined the pain of being a slave. This lady felt it!

Her real name was Isabella Baumfree.

In 1843 she changed her name and began to speak out against slavery. Now she called herself Sojourner Truth. Sojourner means to travel. She told the truth about slavery. Once she visited President Lincoln at the White House!

Sojourner Truth died in 1883. She was born a slave but lived long enough to see the end of slavery. She is buried in a Battle Creek cemetery.

Sojourner Truth traveled and spoke out against slavery. She was a powerful speaker. Courtesy Michigan State Archives.

Laura Haviland

Another brave lady worked with the Underground Railroad. Her name was Laura Haviland. She lived in **Adrian**, Michigan.

At first Laura had a school which helped Black children read and write. Even in Michigan, few African American children could go to school.

Later she helped escaped slaves when they reached Michigan. Still, Laura Haviland did not think this was enough. Finally she traveled to the Southern states. She planned ways to get slaves away from their owners. She did not wait for them to escape on their own. Slave owners were furious. They offered a reward of $3,000 if she could be found and stopped! But Laura Haviland was never caught by the slave owners.

Laura Haviland.
Art by Aaron Zenz.

The idea of slavery divided communities. People argued about it being right or wrong. They argued over what to do about it and sometimes fought about it!

The Crosswhite Story (1847)

It was so nice to live in **Marshall**, Michigan. Lucretia Crosswhite was looking at all the wonderful things in the dry goods store. There were so many colors of cloth and thread. Her father, Adam, had sent her to buy some string. Even though she only needed string, Lucretia loved to look at everything. Since it was 1847, there were not many stores to visit.

As Lucretia ran her finger along the pretty cloth, she heard *the voice*. A stranger was speaking to the storekeeper. The hairs on Lucretia's neck tingled. She had not heard a man speak that way since they lived in Kentucky. Was he from Kentucky? Suddenly Lucretia forgot all about the string. She ran from the store toward home.

Lucretia swung breathlessly through the front door of her house. Her mother grabbed her by her shoulders.

"Lucretia! What is the matter girl?"

"Oh, Mama, I was in the dry goods store. I heard a man speak. I think he is from Kentucky. Perhaps he is looking for us!"

Her mother spoke quietly, "Now Lucretia, you do not know that. Perhaps it means nothing at all."

"But, Mother, I am so worried. Please tell Father."

"Of course I will. You know Father has told the neighbors he will shoot his gun in the air. It will be a warning. They will come to help if there is any trouble."

Lucretia told her brothers and sisters, all four of them. The older ones understood. The younger ones were confused by her worry. Lucretia did not sleep well that night. She had nightmares. Several days later, Lucretia felt a little better.

Then early one cold January morning Lucretia's nightmares became real. There was a terrible pounding

Slave catchers come to Marshall to capture the Crosswhite family. Art by Tim Pickell.

on the front door. Lucretia heard men shouting to be let in. She trembled. Lucretia heard her mother scream, and she jumped out of bed. As soon as her feet touched the cold wood floor, she heard a tremendous bang. A gunshot! Oh dear, that man was from Kentucky! Slave catchers are after us!

You see, Lucretia Crosswhite was born a slave child in Kentucky. She belonged to the Giltner family. When her father learned the Giltners planned to sell his children, they ran away. They traveled across Indiana to Michigan. The family used the Underground Railroad. People fed them and led them to hiding places. Finally the Crosswhites arrived in Marshall, Michigan. After a while, they bought a small home. They wanted to live happily; but now the slave catchers had come.

Lucretia and her brothers and sisters hugged each other. They heard the men shouting and banging on the door. Lucretia began to cry. Would they ever see each other again? She jumped when she heard an awful crash and wood splintering. The door! It had been broken down!

One neighbor heard the gun shot. He jumped on his horse to spread the warning. Moses Patterson rode through Marshall shouting, "Slave catchers at the Crosswhite's. Come quick. Come help."

Even though it was early and cold, people came to the Crosswhite home. The deputy sheriff was with the slave catchers. He told the people the men from Kentucky had papers. Those papers showed they could take the Crosswhites. Some men started to argue with the deputy. They reminded him that slavery was against the law in Michigan. They told the deputy he did not have to help the slave catchers.

Then the deputy spoke loudly, "If you men and women do not get out of the way, I will arrest you." By this time many more people crowded around. Some of the crowd pressed against the deputy and slowly pushed him against the wall. The deputy was about to speak again. He carefully looked at the crowd. He saw 100 or maybe 200 people by now. The deputy thought for a minute. He said, "You men from Kentucky must come with me to my office. Leave this family alone."

One of the slave catchers took out a little notebook and pencil. "I want your names. Tell me who you are! I want to know who will not let us have our property."

The people in the crowd spoke out. One man said, "Charles T. Gorham and write it in capital letters."

"I am Oliver Cromwell Comstock, Junior. Take it down in full so my father will not be held responsible for what I do," said another. Now other people gladly shouted out their names.

The deputy pulled on one of the slave catchers' coat. "Hurry now! Let us leave while we still can."

The crowd shouted, "Arrest THEM deputy! They broke into this man's home. Look, one of them has a pistol. Put THEM in jail!"

The slave catchers left with the deputy sheriff. Now the Crosswhites quickly packed their things. A man took them to his mill. Later they were taken in a wagon to Jackson. The wagon stopped at the train station. Lucretia and her family huddled with the few things they brought with them. Soon they were on a train to Detroit. It was not long before Lucretia, her parents, brothers and sisters were on a boat. They crossed the Detroit River going to Canada.

Lucretia took a long look back at Michigan. She wondered if they would ever come back. She wondered if the slave catchers could find them in Canada. How far must they run to be free?

The next year the men from Kentucky came back to Michigan. This time they went to court. They sued the people who had given their names. They demanded $1925 in payment for the Crosswhite family. That was a lot of money then- much more than the cost of a nice house. Finally the Kentuckians won! The people who gave their names were very worried. But others from Michigan raised money to help pay the cost.

How does the story end? No slave catchers went to Canada after the Crosswhites. Escaped slaves were protected in that country. Several years later some of the Crosswhites came back to Marshall. Adam Crosswhite died in 1878 and is buried in the Marshall cemetery. Some relatives of the Crosswhites still live in Michigan today.

By David B. McConnell with thanks
to Richard W. Carver of Marshall, Michigan.

Arrest THEM!
Put THEM in jail!

The events with the Crosswhite family stirred up trouble in other places. This was one reason new national laws were passed. These laws were called **fugitive** slave laws. They made it more dangerous to help escaped slaves (fugitives). People helping them could face big fines or jail!

Questions to think about

1. Name one core democratic value taken from the Crosswhite family when they were slaves.

2. How did the issue of slavery divide some towns?

3. What did the Underground Railroad do?

4. Who was Sojourner Truth?

5. Who was Laura Haviland?

Brain Stretchers

Slave owners offered a reward of $3,000 to stop Laura Haviland. Imagine you lived at that time and earned $1.28 per day. You work six days a week. How many years' wages is this reward worth?

Words In Action!

Write a journal entry about hiding escaped slaves in your home, or tell about being an escaped slave and trying to find a place to hide.

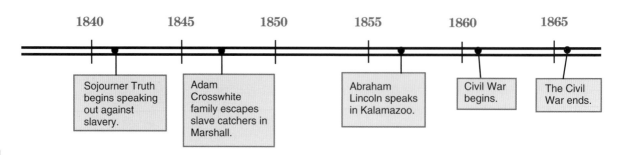

1840	1845	1850	1855	1860	1865

Sojourner Truth begins speaking out against slavery.

Adam Crosswhite family escapes slave catchers in Marshall.

Abraham Lincoln speaks in Kalamazoo.

Civil War begins.

The Civil War ends.

Chapter 5 Lesson 2

Slavery Splits the Nation

Not everyone in Michigan was against slavery. Not everyone liked to see people speak out against it. This was an issue which divided some towns. There were people who felt since the national law allowed slavery, that must mean it was okay. Wasn't helping an escaped slave like helping a robber get away from the sheriff?

In Battle Creek a man named Erastus Hussey began a newspaper. His newspaper had articles against slavery. There were some people who would not read it. Others made fun of those who did. They might say "You ain't one of those anti-slavers are you?" One night someone set his newspaper office on fire. It burned down.

During the 1850s the anger over slavery increased. Each side became violent. New states were starting in the West. Some of these wanted to have slavery. The government in Washington passed laws to allow it. People in the North became upset with their **political parties**.

Soon a war started between the Northern states and the Southern states.

A New Political Party- the Republicans

There was much talk about starting a new political party. Why couldn't there be a party against slavery? Meetings were held to plan that party.

About 1,500 people met at Jackson, Michigan. They decided to form a new party against slavery. They named it the **Republican Party**. The year was 1854.

Soon, people from many states joined the Republican Party. In 1860, Abraham Lincoln ran for president of the United States as a Republican and won.

Abraham Lincoln's victory really bothered many Southern states. In some of those states he was not even on the **ballot**. It seemed no one wanted to try to work together anymore. You were either completely for slavery or completely against it.

We Are Going To Leave!

Several states decided to leave the United States because they wanted to keep slavery. These states were in the South. Nothing like this had ever happened before! Could states decide to leave the country? They thought they could.

Some young people were in the Civil War. This is a drummer boy. The war began in 1861. Art by Theresa Deeter.

This Means War!

In 1861 soldiers from the South attacked a fort belonging to the national government. A war had begun!

This war was called the Civil War. It got this name because it was a war between parts of the same country. The United States was ripping apart.

In this war the North was called the Union side because they wanted the country united again. The South was called the Confederate States of America. A confederacy is a kind of group. Michigan was a part of the Union side.

No battles were fought in Michigan, but we did have some famous people in the war.

Custer Becomes a General

George Custer was a young man from Monroe, Michigan. He left to study at West Point Academy and had just graduated when the war began. He was in the first battle. He was a daring soldier. It was not long before he became a captain in the cavalry.

As he rode he often shouted, "Come on you Wolverines!" Because he was a brave leader, he was finally made a general. He was one of the youngest ever!

General George Custer grew up in Michigan. He commanded a Michigan cavalry unit during the Civil War. Courtesy Michigan State Archives.

Later....

Custer became really famous because of what happened to him after the war. Years later he led troops against tribes in the West. He seemed to think he knew everything. He was not very careful. One day in 1876, he ordered his soldiers to attack a huge group of Indian warriors in Montana. As a result, George Custer and all his men were killed. This was called the Battle of the Little Big Horn.

Women Help

Often the women at home gathered newspapers and blankets to send to the soldiers. Others sent food.

Several Michigan women were nurses during the war. Some of these ladies were Elmira Brainard, Bridget Devins, Annie Etherage, Jennie Hayes, and Julia Wheelock. The nurses often worked under terrible conditions. Sometimes it was dangerous as well.

Several women from Michigan were nurses in the Civil War. Art by Aaron Zenz.

Annie Etherage was about 21 years old when the war began. She volunteered to be a nurse.

Nurses had to be brave to do their work. At the second Battle of Bull Run, Anna was bandaging the wounds of a soldier. He had just whispered his thanks to her. Suddenly he was hit and killed by a cannonball! Once she stopped to talk to a little drummer boy when he was shot. The boy fell against her and dropped dead to the ground.

She was held in the highest regard by Union soldiers. They called her "Gentle Annie."

Besides wounds from battle, the Civil War nurses and doctors had to face a great deal of disease. For every four Michigan soldiers who died from wounds, 10 died from disease! One astonished soldier said this about his group, "We have lost about 30 by disease and have not lost one by the bullet."

Everyone Works to Win

The people of Michigan did more than send soldiers to fight. They mined more copper for brass buttons and other items. They mined more iron to make rifles and cannons. Michigan farmers raised more sheep for their wool. They raised more wheat to feed the soldiers.

Everyone had to work harder to do this. There were fewer people to do the work. Many of the men were away fighting. Women had to run farms while their husbands were away.

The Civil War was very bloody. During the war more than 90,000 Michigan men went to fight. About 4,100 were killed and 10,000 others died of disease.

This African American from Michigan fought in the Civil War. Photo courtesy Michigan State Archives.

It Is Over- Wild With Joy!

One day the war ended. The Union side won. All of the states were again a part of the United States. There was no more slavery. This is what one Michigan soldier said, *"Everyone is wild with joy. As for myself, I cannot write! I cannot talk; only my glad heart cries..."*

These Civil War re-enactors are staging a battle. Photo by Ron Crater.

119

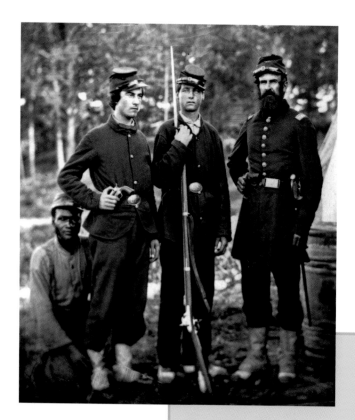

Civil War soldiers
from Michigan.
Courtesy
National Archives,
Washington, D.C.

Then the soldiers came home. They tried to forget the battles and the horrible things they saw. They tried to look to the future. They went back to work on their farms, in the stores, offices and factories.

There was much to do in Michigan because our state was growing. There were homes and factories to build. There were new industries where people could work.

Questions to think about

1. Why did people start the Republican Party?

2. Which Michigan city was the home of General George Armstrong Custer?

3. Choose someone from Michigan who was in the Civil War. Tell what it is you like about them.

Brain Stretchers
At the beginning of the Civil War nearly 750,000 people lived in Michigan. Write a fraction or percentage which shows the number who went to fight.

Words In Action!
Imagine you are at home during the war. Your father has gone away to fight. You must help your mother do all the jobs. Write some diary entries telling what it was like for you.

Chapter 6   Lesson 1

Using Nature's Gifts

What gifts did nature provide Michigan and
how did they help Michigan grow and develop?

A very, very long time ago
there were volcanoes in
Michigan. Courtesy David
McConnell.

What Is Under Our Feet?

Most people never think about what is under the
ground where they walk. There are some valuable
minerals under Michigan's land. We have copper, iron
and salt. The Michigan iron is used to make steel. Oil
and natural gas are there too. The oil is made into gasoline for our cars. Limestone also comes from under the
ground. It is used to make cement. All of these things
are gifts from nature. We call them **natural resources**.

How did these minerals get here? A very long time
ago saltwater seas covered Michigan- mostly the Lower
Peninsula. When the seas dried up they left the minerals
behind. Salt and limestone are two examples.

121

Salt

Most of the Lower Peninsula has thick layers of salt underground. In some places salt was mined. Detroit even had a salt mine. The tunnels of that old mine are still under the city! Some salt was cleaned and used for table salt. You might have eaten a little bit of Michigan on your dinner! We used some to melt ice on our roads.

Limestone

Many places in Michigan have thick layers of **limestone**. Some of the biggest limestone pits are in the northern Lower Peninsula. The white limestone was once the shells of sea creatures. These creatures left behind billions and billions of shells. Over much time, the layers of shells changed into limestone.

Coal and Oil From Really Old Plants

Many plants grew along the shore of the ancient sea. They died and fell to the ground. Great amounts piled up and decayed. The plants became a dark muck. Over a very long time, this plant muck became coal. Some Michigan coal was mined near Jackson and Lansing. The same kind of thing happened to plants growing on the sea bottom. These plants became oil.

Minerals Give Us Jobs

All of these minerals are valuable. Minerals help provide jobs. Where people live and work often depends upon the minerals found in the area.

People from the Upper Peninsula worked in copper and iron mines. That is where those metals are found. There would be no point to dig an iron mine in the Lower Peninsula.

Before we found copper and iron, there were few towns in the Upper Peninsula. When we found these metals in the U.P., many people moved there. They found work in the mines. Others sailed on ships moving the copper and iron on the Great Lakes.

Later, we found oil in the Lower Peninsula. People moved there to drill oil wells. Others found work changing the oil into gasoline and many useful products.

Long after the great saltwater seas, something else happened to Michigan. Great sheets of ice covered the land!

The Big Chill- Mile High Ice

How did we get the Great Lakes? Why do they have those shapes? The story begins thousands of years ago. At that time, the winters got colder and longer. The summers were too short to melt all the snow. The snow became deeper and deeper. It was deepest in the north. After many cold years, it turned into ice and spread south. It became a **glacier**.

Scooped Out the Great Lakes!

The glacier slowly oozed its way toward our area. It came like a

bulldozer. The ice was thousands of feet- maybe a mile- thick! It pushed everything out of its way. The ice scooped out soft places in the ground. These places became the Great Lakes. Finally the glacier started to melt. Melting ice filled all the low places. This water gave the Great Lakes their first big drink!

Thousands of years ago great sheets of ice covered Michigan. The melting ice helped form many of our lakes. Courtesy David McConnell.

What Made Those Hills?

Over thousands of years several glaciers moved across Michigan. As the glaciers moved south, they picked up dirt and stones. Later, they melted and left the dirt and stones behind. This material became the hills we see today.

Most of the glaciers' dirt ended up in the southern Lower Peninsula. This dirt or soil helped to make the crops grow better there. The last glacier melted about 12,000 to 13,000 years ago.

This map shows Michigan's high and low places. The yellow and brown colors are higher land and the dark greens are lower. The highest places are in the western Upper Peninsula. The lowest places are along the Great Lakes, like Lake Erie. Map by Aaron Zenz.

Questions to think about

1. Name four of Michigan's natural resources.

2. Why does Michigan have layers of limestone and salt under it?

3. How did the glaciers of ice help shape Michigan's land?

4. What is one reason the southern Lower Peninsula has good soil for farming?

Brain Stretchers

Make your own crossword puzzle and answer key using words from this lesson.

Words In Action!

Imagine you are a prospector looking for valuable natural resources. Where would you discover these in Michigan? Write about your discovery. Tell where you would invest your money to buy land in Michigan and why.

Time line- here are some events for the next 2 lessons

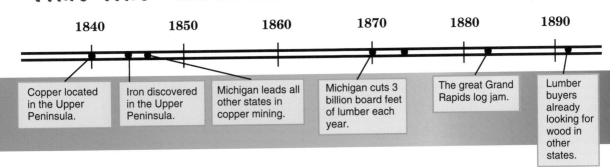

| 1840 | 1850 | 1860 | 1870 | 1880 | 1890 |

Copper located in the Upper Peninsula.

Iron discovered in the Upper Peninsula.

Michigan leads all other states in copper mining.

Michigan cuts 3 billion board feet of lumber each year.

The great Grand Rapids log jam.

Lumber buyers already looking for wood in other states.

Chapter 6 Lesson 2

Two Useful Metals

A piece of shiny Michigan copper.

Copper is not quite like any other metal. When it is clean and shiny, it has its own color. It can be melted and mixed with other metals to make them more useful. It carries electricity very well. So, it is used to make wire and parts for computers, televisions, and electric motors.

The Tribes Were the First Miners

Long before written history, the Native American tribes mined copper in Michigan. They dug the copper on Isle Royale. Isle Royale is a large island far north in Lake Superior. You can still see their small pits in the ground.

The tribes used the copper for spear points and arrowheads. Sometimes other tribes traded for the copper. Pieces of Michigan copper are found buried at old Indian villages far from our state. After a long time, the tribes left Isle Royale. They forgot about the copper.

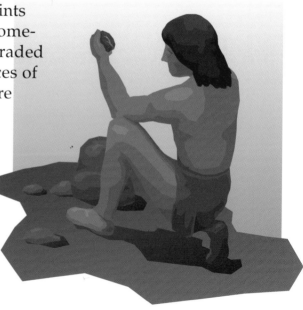

Long ago Native Americans took copper from pits they dug. Art by Aaron Zenz.

Chapter 6 *Using Nature's Gifts*

Search and Discover

In the early days, the state government wanted to learn about the land. It looked for the valuable things nature provided. It hired **Douglass Houghton** to find them. He traveled across Michigan looking for minerals like copper. Copper is valuable because it is so useful. He wrote reports about what he found and where it was.

Many people were interested in Mr. Houghton's reports. The reports said there was copper along the middle of the **Keweenaw Peninsula**. This is the part of the Upper Peninsula that sticks out into Lake Superior. It sounded like a person could become rich from the copper.

The Rush to Find Copper

In 1843, miners started going to the Upper Peninsula to find the copper. Soon, more and more miners arrived. It was a Michigan copper rush!

Some people thought the copper was just lying on the ground. They believed they could pick up the pieces. It was not that easy. Besides, there were terrible swarms of black flies in the summer. In the winter there was bone-chilling cold.

Douglass Houghton studied Michigan's minerals. In 1841 he told about the copper on the Keweenaw Peninsula. Courtesy Michigan State Archives.

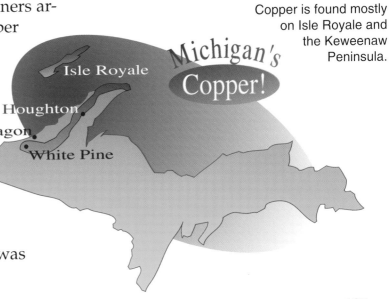

Copper is found mostly on Isle Royale and the Keweenaw Peninsula.

Michigan's Copper!

Isle Royale

Houghton

Ontonagon

White Pine

127

Most Is Far Underground

Most of the copper was found far underground. It was too much work for one miner. Even a dozen could not do it by themselves. The miners formed companies to raise money to buy equipment. The miners needed **capital resources** (equipment) and **human resources** (people working in the mines). Then they were successful in removing the **natural resources** (the copper) from the ground.

The mines went down over 5,000 feet deep! Digging and working such a mine was very expensive. Then the copper had to go by ship to Detroit. That was a long trip. It was over five hundred miles away.

Some pieces of copper were huge! Art by Aaron Zenz.

Nature's "Roadblock!"

Besides being a long trip, there was a major problem. They must unload everything at Sault Ste. Marie. This was necessary because of the swift rapids there. Lake Superior and Lake Huron meet at the Soo. The rapids exist because Lake Superior is about 20 feet higher than Lake Huron. Ships could not sail through the rushing water without being wrecked!

In the Saint Mary's River, the water falls about 20 feet as it rushes from Lake Superior into Lake Huron. Courtesy Library of Congress.

Chapter 6 *Using Nature's Gifts*

The rapids at the Soo were a big problem. The metal was reloaded into other ships and sent on to Detroit. The unloading and reloading took much hard work and long hours.

Finally in 1855 **locks** were built between Lake Superior and Lake Huron. The locks raised and lowered ships between the two big lakes. They were built at Sault Ste. Marie. We call them the **Soo Locks**. The locks were a great help to mining in Michigan. No longer did they need to unload and reload the ships.

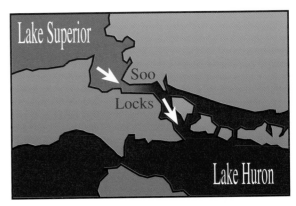

The Soo Locks are between Michigan and Canada. Map by Aaron Zenz.

Copper Mined in Michigan

Mining copper was an important activity in Michigan for a long time. How much copper was mined in Michigan in 1889? More copper was mined here than in any other state or country!

They Came To Work!

Many people moved into this part of the state to mine copper. Once, one mine alone had over 2,000 workers. New towns began. People even came from other countries to work in the mines.

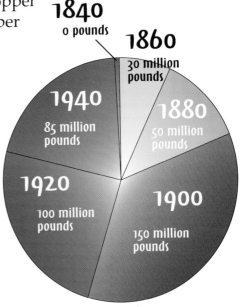

It Becomes Too Expensive

As the years went by, more of the mines closed. The last one closed in 1995. Today there are no more copper mines operating in Michigan. Copper is still far underground, but it is too expensive to get out.

The amount of copper mined in Michigan for six different years.

Iron ore being loaded onto a ship at Marquette. Courtesy Michigan State Archives.

Iron- Everyone Uses It

Iron **ore** was found in Michigan soon after copper mining began. Iron is the backbone of industry. It is used to make steel. It is used for tall buildings, cars, and nails.

A surveyor named William Burt traveled to the Upper Peninsula. In 1844, he and his crew were surveying near the middle of the Peninsula. Mr. Burt was trying to make good maps. For his work it was important to use a compass. He needed to know which way was north and which was south.

My Compass Is Crazy!

One day, his compass needle did not point north at all! His men found it was pointing toward large pieces of iron ore instead.

This surprised everyone. No one in Michigan had any idea the state had this useful mineral. Finding iron ore was indeed a very nice surprise!

Michigan's Iron!

Ironwood
Negaunee
Marquette
Ishpeming
Iron River
Iron Mountain

Thank You For Helping- maybe!

Some men from Jackson, Michigan wanted to start a mine. They were interested in the valuable minerals of the U.P. They did not know much about mining, though. Nor did they know exactly where to go. On the way, they met an Ojibwa chief. The chief's name was **Marji-Gesick.** The chief took them to a hill which sparkled in the sun. It was full of iron ore!

The men told the chief they would say thanks by giving him **stock** in their mine. He had been a great help!

Years went by. After the old chief died, his daughter wanted that stock in the iron mine. Her name was **Charlotte Kawbawgam** or Laughing Whitefish. The mining company made excuses about why they should keep the stock. They did not want to share the wealth anymore.

Charlotte went to court and fought hard for several years. Finally, the court told the company to give her the stock.

Today, Michigan has only two working iron mines. However, they can still produce much iron ore. These mines are not far from Marquette. They supply an important part of all the iron mined in the United States. Over the years workers have mined more than one billion tons of iron ore in the Upper Peninsula!

Charlotte Kawbawgam (Laughing Whitefish) went to court to get her father's stock in the Jackson Iron Mine. He was the man who led the miners to the iron!

A miner with a one-man drill. The miners only have candles for light in the dark mine. Imagine how hard it must have been to see!

131

Questions to think about

1. Explain where copper and iron are found in Michigan.

2. Why are copper and iron useful?

3. In which ways did the discovery of copper and iron help the Upper Peninsula grow and develop?

4. About which year was the most copper mined in Michigan?

5. Write the names Douglass Houghton and Marji-Gesick on your paper. Next to each name write the mineral that person helped discover.

Brain Stretchers
Make a map which shows where several of Michigan's minerals are found. Decide which peninsula has the most valuable natural resources and explain why. (Maybe there is no right or wrong answer.)

Words In Action!
Use your imagination. Tell what it was like working in a Michigan mine 100 years ago.

Today most iron ore is shipped like little marbles. This is what fills many of the huge ships on the Great Lakes.
Photo by Dave McConnell.

Chapter 6 Lesson 3

Down Go the Tall Trees

What did Michigan gain and what did Michigan lose
from the way it used its trees?

Everyone Wanted Lumber!

"Timberrr!" shouts the log cutter. The big tree
slowly falls to the ground and hits with a crash. Men
scurry around to cut off limbs and saw the trunk into
logs. Smell that fresh sawdust!

The lumber days were exciting times for
Michigan. There were some mighty interesting
people working the woods. They had nicknames
like Dynamite Jack, Chris Crosshaul, Cedar Root
Charley, and Slabwood Johnson. They were tough
and worked hard.

Once Wasted- Now Valuable

The first farmers got rid of trees just to plant
crops. There were many more trees than they could
ever use. Many were cut and burned. The supply of
trees was much greater than the demand. At that
time, trees were not worth very much.

After the Civil War, demand increased. Buildings
were destroyed in the fighting. Wood was needed to
rebuild. People wanted new homes in fast-growing
cities like Chicago. Others moved to the western
states. There were not many trees there. Everyone
wanted more wood in the 1860s and 1870s!

Earlier, Maine and New York had been the leading
lumbering states. Now their supply of trees was
shrinking. Michigan had plenty of trees.

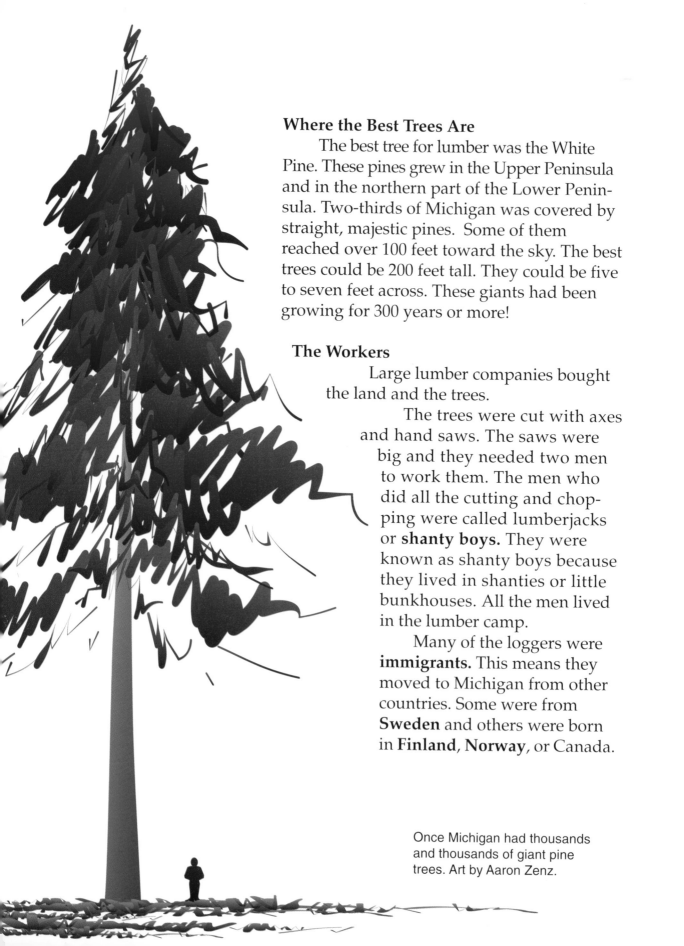

Where the Best Trees Are

The best tree for lumber was the White Pine. These pines grew in the Upper Peninsula and in the northern part of the Lower Peninsula. Two-thirds of Michigan was covered by straight, majestic pines. Some of them reached over 100 feet toward the sky. The best trees could be 200 feet tall. They could be five to seven feet across. These giants had been growing for 300 years or more!

The Workers

Large lumber companies bought the land and the trees.

The trees were cut with axes and hand saws. The saws were big and they needed two men to work them. The men who did all the cutting and chopping were called lumberjacks or **shanty boys.** They were known as shanty boys because they lived in shanties or little bunkhouses. All the men lived in the lumber camp.

Many of the loggers were **immigrants.** This means they moved to Michigan from other countries. Some were from **Sweden** and others were born in **Finland**, **Norway**, or Canada.

Once Michigan had thousands and thousands of giant pine trees. Art by Aaron Zenz.

Often a Winter Job

At first, the work was done in the winter. It was easier to move the big logs over the ice. The big logs were put on sleds. Horses or oxen pulled the sleds. Still, it was too far to pull the logs all the way to the **sawmill.** The shanty boys often used rivers to carry the logs.

Rivers Move the Logs

Logs float, so rivers were a perfect way to move them to the sawmills. The shanty boys worked all winter. They cut the trees down and dragged the logs to a river. The logs were stacked up along the bank. The stack grew each day until spring. After the ice melted, the rivers were high with water. Then the rivers flowed their fastest.

This is what a sawmill looked like in the 1880s. See the huge spinning saw blade! Courtesy Michigan State Archives. Photo colorized by Robert Morrison.

All at once the logs were pushed into the river. Away they went! The lumbermen went along with them. Some men called themselves **river hogs**. These men balanced on logs as they floated along. They wore boots with sharp spikes to help them stay on the logs. What did these men with the strange name do? The river hogs kept the logs from piling up into a log jam. If a log jam started, the whole river would fill with logs for miles.

Lumber camps grew up along the rivers. The **Saginaw River** Valley was the first main lumbering region. Logging continued there until the early 1900s. Once, there were 112 sawmills between Saginaw and Bay City!

A two person crosscut saw. Art by David McConnell.

The other major lumber area was along the Muskegon River. As the years passed, logging moved further north and into the Upper Peninsula.

Many towns started in the northern part of Michigan during the lumber years. The towns began as people moved north to cut the trees. Here is a list of some of Michigan's lumber towns.

Alpena, Baraga, Bay City, Cheboygan,
Escanaba, Manistee, Manistique
Menominee, Muskegon, Saginaw, Traverse City

The Life of a Shanty Boy

The day began in the cold and dark before the sun was up. Men drove sprinkler sleighs which held large tanks of water. The water coated the trail and formed a slick layer of ice. The ice on the roads made it easier for the sleds full of logs.

Plenty of good food kept the shanty boys working hard to cut the trees. Courtesy David McConnell. Photo colorized by Robert Morrison.

The cook and the cook's helpers began work early. It was a big job to make breakfast. Bread, biscuits, cookies, and pies were put into the oven. Doughnuts were fried. Pancake batter was mixed and put into the skillet. Gallons of coffee and tea were brewed. All of this cooking was done on a huge wood burning stove.

The shanty boys were up and out of their bunks before daylight. They gathered in the cookhouse and ate the huge breakfast. Talking was always forbidden while eating. It was an old loggers' custom.

Chapter 6   *Using Nature's Gifts*

The shanty boys or lumberjacks worked hard all day. Often they would not come back to the camp until dark. They worked six days a week. Their pay was about one dollar a day!

Paul Bunyan and Tall Tales

During their day off, the Shanty boys told legends and stories. One of their favorite stories was about **Paul Bunyan**. Each time the story was told, something was added to it. Soon, the stories were hard to believe, but that just made them better. They might say Paul Bunyan was 12 feet, 11 inches tall without his socks!

Did you know Paul Bunyan had a pet ox called Babe? Babe was huge and she was colored blue! Paul found Babe frozen in the ice of Lake Superior. Babe had turned blue from the cold!

The Trees Fall Faster

At first people said Michigan's trees would last *forever*! As time passed, the loggers discovered new ways to cut the trees faster. They built better equipment.

A wagon maker from Manistee invented **big wheels.** These were really BIG wheels! Logs were chained to the axle in the middle. Now horses or oxen could drag the logs. They could be moved in the summer or winter.

Someone else thought of using small railroads with

This is a large sawmill from the lumber days. See the many logs floating in the river. There are two sailing ships waiting to be loaded with boards. Courtesy Michigan State Archives.

narrow tracks. New saws were made for the sawmills. The logs were cut into boards faster than ever. More trees were cut than ever before.

How Much Was Cut?

How much lumber came from Michigan? This was big business from 1840 to 1900. In those years about 170,000,000,000 **board feet** were cut. What does a big number like that mean? That is more than enough wood to build a floor over the entire state! Rhode Island could be covered with the leftovers!

The picture shows land after the loggers left. These are pine tree stumps. Without trees and plants to hold the topsoil in place, wind and rain washed it away. The land was no longer very useful for farming. Courtesy Michigan State Archives.

Oops- They Forgot to Plant More!

Today we do not see many really tall trees in Michigan. The lumberjacks did not think about planting more. There was very little **conservation.** Lumbering was done with little thought about the future. They cut all the trees for quick money. They did not think about saving any for tomorrow.

It took nature a long time to grow a state full of trees! It will take a long time for the giant trees to grow back. We will all have to help them grow. This means

everyone should be careful in the woods. We should not cut down young trees. We should not leave camp fires burning. Forest fires can kill many of the trees again!

The Last Giants

There are only a few places where the original white pines are still standing. One is at **Hartwick Pines State Park** near Grayling. Most people will never see one of these 200-foot giants unless they visit the park.

There is still some lumbering in Michigan. Now most trees are changed into pulp to make paper.

Questions to think about

1. At one time, people burned trees just to get rid of them. What changes caused the trees to become valuable?

2. What kind of tree was used so much during our lumber days?

3. Why were the rivers important to early lumbering?

4. Who is an immigrant?

5. Did the trees last as long as people first thought they would? What things changed?

Brain Stretchers
Make an acrostic poem using words from Michigan's logging days.

Writing Activity
Suppose you could send a letter back in time to one of the logging companies. Try to help them understand why they should plant new trees. Tell them how this will help them and other people as well.

Chapter 6 Lesson 4

The sawmills along the Grand River brought furniture makers. Good wood was close by. The flowing river gave their factories water power.

One year a small company began in Grand Rapids. It did not make furniture. Its workers did use wood though. They used it to make carpet sweepers. These sweepers were muscle-powered. They were pushed across the floor. Here is the story of that company and the people behind it.

You Can Do It Mrs. Bissell! (1889)

Story illustrated by Don Ellens

My name is Mary Maud Vandenberg. I am 10 years old and live in Grand Rapids, Michigan. I come from a big family– quite a big family actually. I share my parents with nine brothers and sisters! With so many children, Ma and Pa are often short of money. That means those of us who are old enough, work to help out.

Some places with jobs for children were dirty or not safe. Father said he would not have us labor all day making cigars. Mother said there were too many children hurt in the furniture factories.

I was very lucky. One of mother's friends found a place for me. Now I work after school and on Saturdays at the Bissell home. They are very nice to me.

You have heard of the Bissells haven't you? They have a big business making carpet sweepers here in Grand Rapids. They say Mr. Bissell thought of the idea all by himself. Lots of ladies buy his sweepers. Those sweepers save so much time. Now, no one has to haul all of the carpets out each spring and beat them! Just push a Bissell sweeper over the rugs every few days, and they are clean.

The Bissells just bought a big, beautiful house. The house is so pretty and has lots of rooms. It is grand to work there.

I dust the furniture, sweep the floors, and put the dishes on the table for supper. If it is cold, I bring wood for each of the six fire-places. I am paid 25¢ a day! The money is a big help at home.

A Bissell carpet sweeper.
Art by Don Ellens.

Lately it has been very sad at the Bissells. Mr. Bissell died of pneumonia. He was only 46 years old. Everyone was crying. Mrs. Bissell, Anna, is heartbroken. His death was mentioned in all the newspapers. Many people have come to comfort the Bissells. I helped hang up the visitors' hats and coats.

An important man has just come to the house. He has stepped out of his carriage. What a fine black horse he has! I must hurry to the door...

"Good afternoon, sir! May I please take your hat and coat. Thank you, sir. Mrs. Bissell is in the library. May I show you the way?" I think the visitor is Mr. Clark, the Bissell's lawyer.

I took the caller to the library. "Mrs. Bissell, a gentleman is here to see you."

He walked in and gave her arm a little squeeze. "Anna, I know Melville's funeral was only a few days

ago. But, there are things to do. We must talk about the business. If you can't find a good man to take charge, I think you should sell."

Anna Bissell just looked at him with sad eyes. "But we have both worked so hard at the business. Perhaps I can carry on somehow?"

Mr. Clark continued, "Now Anna. You are not thinking clearly. How can a woman run a business? And it is a big business too. Just think of the troubles you had after the fire five years ago. Suppose something terrible like that happened again? No bank would give a woman a big loan to rebuild the factory! Let me write a letter to the Goshen Sweeper Company. Let me see how much they will offer."

"Oh, I suppose. You are probably right. I shall think about it."

"Well then, Anna. I think you are coming to your senses. Your place is home with the children. Running a business brings many worries. I will be at my office if you need me. Good day!"

Mr. Clark walked briskly out of the library. As he passed me, he pulled a cigar from his coat pocket. I just stood near the door. Mrs. Bissell sat there and looked like she was ready to cry. I slowly walked over to her.

I said, " I don't think that man is very nice."

"Mr. Clark? Oh, Mary Maud, he is just trying to do his job. He is trying to do the best thing for us."

"But if you don't want to sell your company, why should you? You are smart. At least I have always

thought so. You know all about the sweeper business."
Anna Bissell had a little tremble. Then I blurted out,
"Mrs.Bissell, you CAN do it! I just know you can!"

Mrs. Bissell looked up at me. A bit of a smile
slowly came to her face. Her eyes twinkled. She
slapped her hand down on the desk. "Mary Maud, I
do think you might be right. You are so sweet to say
so. You don't have to be a man to run a business!"
Mrs. Bissell gave me a big hug. She said, "I have
some work to do and had best get started!"

Mary and Mrs. Bissell.
Art by Don Ellens.

Within four years Anna Bissell's company was making 1,000 sweepers a day! She started selling Bissell sweepers around the world. Britain became her second largest market. She kept the company going even after vacuum cleaners were invented. Mrs. Bissell was always concerned about her workers. Once she had a party for them at her home. Four hundred people came.

Anna Bissell ran the Bissell company for 30 years- from 1889 to 1919. She died in 1934 and Grand Rapids felt it was a great loss.

Questions to think about

1. Compare what life could be like for a 10 year old in 1889 and today.

2. What did the Bissell company make?

3. What did Mr. Clark think about Mrs. Bissell running the company on her own?

4. Did Anna Bissell succeed in running the company? Use facts from the story to explain your answer.

Brain Stretchers
The story tells about two places young people might work in 1889. Think of at least six more places on your own.

Writing Activity
Write an essay on how attitudes about women and children working have changed in the last 100 years. Use information in this story and facts you already know.

Chapter 7 Lesson 1

On the Move-
Rivers, Roads, Ships, Trains, and Cars

How important is transportation in our lives?

Today we can get in touch with others instantly. We can phone, fax, e-mail, and have video conferences. Michigan astronaut Jerry Linenger spent five months in the MIR space station. Each day he was able to e-mail a letter to his son! Not too long ago it was not like this at all. Getting in touch could take days, weeks or months. Travel was slow.

The ability to **communicate**, to travel, and to ship supplies affects how we work with each other. It affects where we live and our jobs.

Travel Long Ago

What was travel like when Father Marquette came from France in 1666? The trip on a sailing ship took six weeks to cross the Atlantic Ocean. After a week or so, all the fresh food was gone. Soon insects got into the food which was left. Yuck! Many passengers and crew became sick and some died.

Mail Service

"Did you bring any letters from home? Did you?" That is what people asked Marquette as soon as he

For almost 200 years sailing ships brought people and supplies to Michigan. Art by Aaron Zenz.

145

stepped off the ship. That was the way letters reached people. There was no post office in those times.

Lakes and Rivers Are the Highways

During the 1600s, the 1700s, and the early part of the 1800s, almost all travel was by water. Using rivers and lakes for travel worked well for a long time. Then in the 1820s and 1830s settlers moved to Michigan. They wanted to buy cheap land and the cheap land was away from the towns. The settlers wanted better ways to reach this land.

A Real Need For Roads

Most Michigan settlers came to Detroit first. The early roads helped them head west. Later, a few roads went north. They reached Pontiac, Flint, Saginaw and Bay City.

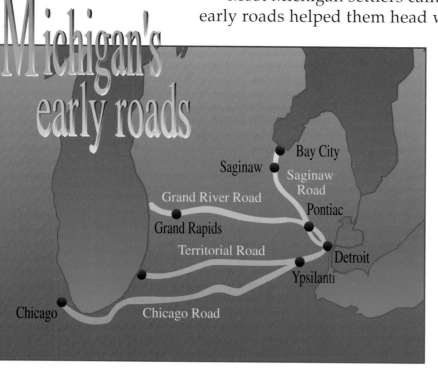

Early Roads Were An Adventure!

To us, an early road might have looked more like a path. It was not paved. It was a mess in rainy weather. Wagons often became stuck in the mud.

A map of Michigan's first roads.

Who Built Early Roads?

At first, the government did not build many roads. Some of the roads were private. Those were called **toll roads**. Each wagon driver and horse rider paid a fee or toll to use the road. The money went to the people who built the road.

Some owners of toll roads tried to improve them. They laid logs or wooden boards on the ground, and called them **plank roads**.

Plank roads were nice for a few months. Then the boards began to come apart and warp. These roads were famous for being bumpy. It is said traveling on them could shake out a person's false teeth!

How Fast Did They Go?

How fast could people travel? This is what one early settler said. In 1828 Abraham Edwards brought his wife and 10 children on the **Chicago Road**.

Plank roads were covered with boards. Soon they became very rough and bumpy. Art by Aaron Zenz.

*...The first night from Detroit we slept at TenEyck's tavern, at **Dearborn**. The second night at Sheldon's (A small village about 6 miles east of **Ypsilanti**.) The third night two miles west of Ypsilanti. From this camp we left the settlements.... and did not meet a white face for eighteen days.*

Look at a map. How far is it from Detroit to Dearborn? If you rode in a car all day, how far would you travel?

Stagecoaches took travelers from city to city before the railroads were built.

Stagecoaches were not just "out West." Michigan had them too. Stagecoach lines reached many cities. Most of the stagecoach lines started in the 1830s and 1840s. Riding in a stagecoach was not any better than riding in a wagon. By the 1860s trains were replacing the stagecoaches.

Trains!

The first trains were slow. They went about 25 miles an hour. They were still much faster than a wagon. Courtesy Michigan State Archives.

Michigan had its first railroad in 1836. It went from Toledo to Adrian. On the opening day, the "train" started toward Adrian- pulled by horses! This railroad did not get its engine until the next year.

The first railroads seem like something to laugh

about. Still, they were exciting for the times. The trip from Detroit to Ypsilanti took two and a half hours instead of two and a half days! The high cost of shipping had made products very expensive. Now prices began to fall.

Big Plans

In the early years, the state government decided to build

railroads and canals. People believed these projects would help settlers, farmers, and businesses. Transportation was very important to help Michigan grow.

The projects were hard to build and cost much money. The governor borrowed five million dollars. Before long, the money was gone and the projects were not finished. Everyone was very upset.

Never Again!

Laws were changed so the state government was not allowed to borrow money for big projects. The partly-finished railroad track was sold to some railroad companies. The companies finished the railroad lines in a few years.

Trains, Trains Everywhere

It is hard to realize the importance of early railroads. Every city and town wanted to be on one. Places not on railroads felt left out. Businesses could not get supplies. They could not ship products. People could not reach the town easily. Cities on rail lines grew. Those without railroads did not.

In 1836, Michigan had about 30 miles of railroad. By the year 1900, Michigan had over 10,000 miles of railroads! People could travel almost any place by train. That was good, since there were still very few roads.

A train engine of the 1860s to 1880s.

Today, there are only a few passenger trains connecting just the largest cities. In 1900 there were trains to almost every town in the state. People often went to work on trains. They used trains to go to larger cities to shop. Some cities had 50 or more trains stop each day!

Big Ships and the Great Lakes

Come to one of Michigan's port cities about 100 years ago. Look at all the ships! Smoke is puffing up from the steamships. Big white sails hang on the masts of the sailing ships. People are hurrying this way and that. Workers are rolling big barrels onto ships. Some ships are stacked high with boards from nearby sawmills.

Many passengers once traveled on Great Lakes ships. In this photo people are boarding two steamers at Port Huron, Michigan.

Photo courtesy Library of Congress. Colorized by Robert Morrison.

For about 100 years Michigan port cities were very busy places. From 1830 to about 1930 thousands and thousands of passengers and tons of products traveled by ship. People often took vacations on ships. Ships took people from crowded cities to relaxing **resorts.**

From Sail to Steam Engines

At first, most of the ships used sails. The wind moved them from place to place. Of course, the wind does not always blow when it is needed. Sometimes it blows too hard. Sailors wanted power which they controlled. Steam

Long ago, many people traveled the Great Lakes on ships with paddle wheels.
Art by David McConnell.

150

engines were the answer. Soon more ships used steam engines and fewer used sails. A number of early ships did not use propellers. They were pushed through the water by big paddle wheels on each side. It is very unusual to see that kind of ship today.

Mostly Cargo Now

After better roads and faster trains were built, people used ships less. Now most ships on the Great Lakes only carry cargo. The only ships people use are **ferries**. These are ships which take people and sometimes their cars. Ferries take people to places like Mackinac Island and Beaver Island. One ferry even takes people across Lake Michigan to Wisconsin.

Today's huge **freighters** carry iron ore, coal, limestone and other material. Some of these ships are 1,000 feet long! These ships are built just for those cargoes. They are called **bulk cargoes** because they can be poured into the ship. Such cargoes are quickly unloaded using special equipment.

Most of the ships carrying bulk cargoes are not built to go across the ocean. Other ships do that work. Many of those ships stop at Michigan ports. If you go near the ports you can see their foreign flags and their strange names.

This is what one of the Great Lakes cargo ships looks like. Some people call them freighters. This ship is the *Algogulf*. Courtesy of the Algoma Central Marine.

Questions to think about

1. If you wished to travel from Detroit to Bay City in the year 1750, what would you probably use? What might you use in 1850?

2. Tell what you know about toll roads and plank roads.

3. How did better ways of travel and shipping help Michigan grow?

4. Name some cargoes Great Lakes ships carry today.

Brain Stretchers
Design a chart or graph to show how people were able to travel faster during the years covered in this chapter.

Words In Action!
Choose a method of travel you find interesting. Make an imaginary trip between two places in Michigan. Tell what it would be like to make this trip. Remember to tell **when** you are taking your trip.

This is the U.S. Coast Guard icebreaker *Mackinac*.

Chapter 7 Lesson 2

Two Helpful Inventors

No Lights or Electricity!

Has the power ever gone off in your home? Did it last for a long time? Soon you probably wondered what you could do. Nothing worked anymore. Maybe one of your parents lit a kerosene lamp. Before the 1880s everyone lived without electric lights and electricity! Someone who grew up in Michigan helped give us these things. It was **Thomas Edison** from **Port Huron**.

When he was seven, Edison moved from Ohio to Port Huron. That was in 1854. His father started a feed and grain store there.

His First Job

In 1859, Port Huron was buzzing with excitement. The railroad from Detroit was coming to town. Tom heard some railroad officials talking. They were looking for a boy to sell newspapers on the train. He walked up to the men and boldly asked "How would I do?" He got the job!

A Good Use For Free Time

He rode the train from Port Huron to Detroit each day. Once he reached Detroit he waited eight hours for it to go back. He could have gotten into trouble with so much free time. Instead, he spent the time exploring the city. One day he saw a sign for the Detroit Free Library. Now he spent his eight hours reading! He soon found

Young Thomas Edison. Art by George Rasmussen.

the books about science to be the most interesting. Thomas Edison began to do **experiments**.

Quick Action!

On an August day in 1862, Tom was waiting for a train. He was at the **Mt. Clemens** station. He heard the whistle. Suddenly he saw the station agent's little boy playing in the gravel— right between the tracks! Edison made a mad dash and grabbed the boy. The engine was close. It was so close it knocked off the heel of Tom's shoe. The little boy was almost killed!

Learning About a New Invention

The boy's father was so grateful. He told Tom he would teach him to be a **telegraph** operator. Tom Edison thought that would be great.The telegraph was a new **invention**. It allowed messages to be sent on wires long distances. Edison spent many hours at Mt. Clemens learning to use the telegraph.

A telegraph. Art by Aaron Zenz.

Tom Edison got a job as a telegraph operator with the railroad. He left Port Huron and went to Adrian. He learned more and more about the telegraph. Soon he was thinking of ways to make it work better. In 1869 Thomas Edison sold his first invention.He was paid $40,000!

Some Great Inventions

He built a lab in New Jersey. Now he could spend all his time working on inventions. One of those inventions was the light bulb. Another was the record player. Thomas Edison became one of America's greatest inventors. Today, Edison's lab has been moved to Greenfield Village in Dearborn. You can visit it and see where he worked.

A Well Oiled Machine

Thomas Edison was not the only inventor to live in Michigan. **Elijah McCoy** was another. Mr. McCoy also worked on railroads. Elijah McCoy was the son of slaves who had escaped to Canada. After going to school in Canada, he spent five years studying in Scotland. Elijah was very smart.

One of Thomas Edison's early light bulbs. Art by Aaron Zenz.

Too Smart to Shovel Coal

When he was 21 years old he came to Michigan and moved to **Ypsilanti.** He worked as a **fireman** with the Michigan Central Railroad. Elijah McCoy was too smart to shovel coal all day. He always watched to find ways to make the engines work better. He knew engines would stop without oil. The oil kept the parts sliding back and forth smoothly.

Keep the Engines Going

Elijah McCoy's first invention was a better device to oil train en-

Elijah McCoy. Art by Aaron Zenz.

A railroad engine oiler. Art by Aaron Zenz.

gines. It was a great improvement. He **patented** his idea on July 23, 1872.

Other people copied Elijah's idea. That was not nice. But often their copies did not work very well. Engineers soon asked, "Is that the real McCoy?"

During his career Elijah McCoy made 78 inventions. Most of Mr. McCoy's inventions help oil machines. Remember Elijah McCoy each February during Black History Month in Michigan.

Questions to think about

1. Name two ways Thomas Edison used his free time when he was young.

2. Name two things invented by Thomas Edison.

3. How did Elijah McCoy's inventions help machines run well?

4. Make a time line with the events mentioned in this lesson. Include something about both inventors.

Brain Stretchers

The things invented by Edison and McCoy really changed life for people in those times. Name something you think might be invented in your life. How will it change the way people live?

Words In Action!

Write an article for the 1862 Mt. Clemens newspaper. Tell about Thomas Edison saving the boy at the railroad station. Start your article with a headline. You might want to draw a picture for the article too.

Chapter 7 Lesson 3

Wow! What a Car! *(1902)*

This story is illustrated by Mark Koenig.

I am George May. My brother and I work at the race track in **Grosse Pointe**. Yes, it is the place near Detroit where the horses race.

I bring in straw and spread it around. We both clean up after the horses. There can be lots to clean up after all those horses! Sometimes the smell gets to me, but horses are everywhere. There are horses on the main streets. Horses on the side streets. Horses in the stables. You just have to get used to the mess and the smell. Everyone has a horse. Don't you?

The last year or so the racetrack has something new. They have **automobile** races. They buzz those horseless carriages around until most of them break down.

Hey, listen. Some men are bringing an automobile in now. I am going to go over and see who they are. . .

"Say mister, who are you? I am George."

"Well, sonny, my name's Oldfield- **Barney Oldfield**. You must have heard about me."

I thought for a second. I had never heard his name before. I didn't want to sound like a dummy. I decided to play up to the man. "So, you are that famous fellow." I said.

George watches as the race car is unloaded.

"Sonny, you must read the papers!" With that remark he slapped me on the back so hard I nearly lost my breath. "Yup, I am that famous bicycle racin' fellow. I rode 'em all. Made a bit of a name for myself, I did."

Here come two other men.

"Son, this is **Tom Cooper** and **Henry Ford**. They talked me into riding this horseless carriage contraption. Mr. Ford built it. Only thing is I had better practice some. See, I don't know how to drive yet!"

I was afraid Mr. Oldfield might slap me on the back again. I quickly moved over and walked around the 'contraption.' It was an odd thing to see. Reminded me of a bed frame with an engine on one end and the seat on the other. A big engine was bolted to one end of a heavy open frame. Toward the back there was a single seat. . . no body, no doors, no windshield. . . and to steer there was this handle. I did not know what to call it.

I asked why they used that sort of steering handle.

Mr. Ford spoke, "When the machine is making high speed the operator cannot see with all the dust. He can't tell whether he is going straight. This way he can look at the steering handle. . . if it is set straight across, he is alright!"

I asked them what they called their race car. Mr. Ford said he named it the "999." He named it after the high-speed train.

The men started the car. Wow! The roar alone was half enough to kill a man. It almost completely killed a boy like me! Henry Ford had created a monster. The ground even shook.

Mr. Ford and Mr. Cooper gave Barney Oldfield some tips on how to drive it. Then he was off!

Barney Oldfield tries
out the race car.

After a few laps he pulled up in front of us. Mr. Oldfield now looked like "Mr. Oilfield." There were many leaks around the engine. He had oil splattered all over his face, his goggles, his shirt. Any inch that didn't have oil was covered with dust!

Then Mr. Oldfield spoke, "Whew. I cannot quite describe it. Going over Niagara Falls would be a treat after that ride. . . This **chariot** may kill me. . . but I might as well be dead as dead broke!"

Henry Ford and his friend, Tom Cooper, practiced with the 999. But they were afraid to drive it in a race. That's when they thought of Barney Oldfield. It was said, "Nothing's too fast for him. . . He'll try anything once." The 999's engine had about 100 horsepower. That made it the most powerful engine built then.

I went to that race to see the 999. It was October 25, 1902. Four cars raced for five miles. That day Barney Oldfield made an American speed record in Henry Ford's car. He went the five miles in five minutes and 28 seconds. That is almost 60 miles per hour. When the race was over, the crowd carried Barney Oldfield around on their shoulders.

Barney Oldfield's success attracted investors to Henry Ford. That is why the car was built. The investors bought stock in his third auto company. The first two companies went broke. They started the Ford Motor Company in June, 1903. The money from the investors paid for wages, parts and supplies.

None of the investors was rich. One man sold coal. Another man worked in the coal office. One lady was a school teacher.

One person borrowed the money from his father. A fifth person borrowed money on some land he owned. The school teacher only had $200. She used $100 to buy Ford stock. Sixteen years later Henry Ford bought it back and paid her $260,000. Everyone else became millionaires!

Questions to think about

1. What did George think about Henry Ford's race car?

2. Was Barney Oldfield an experienced race car driver when he decided to drive the 999?

3. What was the most important reason Henry Ford built this race car?

4. What risk did investors in the Ford company take? What rewards did they get for taking this risk?

Brain Stretchers

In 1900 the car business was new and risky. Tell about a business today which is just as new and risky. Do you think it will change our lives as much as the car business did?

Words In Action!

Pretend to be a newspaper reporter. Write an article about Barney Oldfield and the 999 race for your paper. You may draw a picture to go with your article.

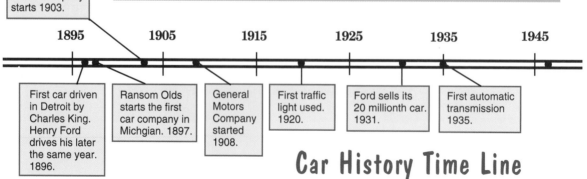

Barney Oldfield races the 999 in 1902. Ford Motor Company starts 1903.

| 1895 | 1905 | 1915 | 1925 | 1935 | 1945 |

First car driven in Detroit by Charles King. Henry Ford drives his later the same year. 1896.

Ransom Olds starts the first car company in Michgian. 1897.

General Motors Company started 1908.

First traffic light used. 1920.

Ford sells its 20 millionth car. 1931.

First automatic transmission 1935.

Car History Time Line

Henry Ford's 999 race car driven by Barney Oldfield in 1902.

Chapter 7 Lesson 4

Changing From Horses to Cars

Many Horses

Let us go back to the old days. For trips closer to home, people rode in wagons or buggies pulled by horses. Most people had a stable or barn and kept a couple of horses. Someone had to feed, brush, and take care of the horses. Maybe that would be someone like you! Keeping horses was a lot of work and bother.

A Horseless Carriage!

About the year 1900, several people had ideas for an easier way to travel. They started to build horseless carriages. Of course, *something* had to make the carriage go. Some had gasoline engines. Others used little steam engines. Most people thought these little horseless carriages were just toys. Toys for rich people!

Three Michigan men thought horseless carriages could be a serious way to travel. These men were Henry Ford, Billy Durant and Ransom Olds. They all tried to make a car that would run well. They each started a company to make cars.

Ransom Olds at home with his family in Lansing about 1900. Courtesy Michigan State Archives. Photo colorized by Robert Morrison.

The First Car Company Here

A man named Ransom Olds had a factory at Lansing. He made small cars there. This was the first company to make cars in Michigan. The Olds company was started in 1897. He made a car called the "Curved-dash Olds." By 1900, this car was so popular songs were written about it! In 1903 one of these cars cost $650.00. People thought it was sensational! Today we might think it was more like a big riding lawn mower without a blade!

This is what Mr. Olds said in 1904. "I predict that the automobile business will be one of the greatest industries this country has ever seen." He sold 5,500 cars that year.

Oldsmobile

The Oldsmobile Curved Dash Runabout. It was built from 1900 to 1904.

Today, It Is the Biggest

Billy Durant moved in 1872 to be with his grandparents in Flint, Michigan. As a young man he had an idea for a new carriage. He started a carriage company in 1886. It was not long before he had the largest carriage company in the world! Flint, Michigan was known as the city that put the world on wheels—carriage wheels.

Billy Durant could see changes coming. New ideas and technology would change the ways people traveled. He felt the horseless carriage would be the thing of the future. So, he started a car company which is now called General Motors. That was in 1908. Today GM is one of the biggest companies in the world. It still has factories in Flint.

William (Billy) Durant began the General Motors Company in 1908. That was the same year Henry Ford started making the Model T. Courtesy Michigan State Archives.

General Motors

It was not easy to start such a large company. The company had to get big loans from banks. After a while, the bankers did not like the way Mr. Durant ran the company. They decided they could do a better job themselves. They told Billy Durant to leave General Motors.

Over the years Billy Durant lost much of his money. When Mr. Durant was an old man he worked in a Flint bowling alley. Many people had forgotten who he was. Billy Durant, however, had really helped put the world on wheels!

Henry Ford

Henry Ford did not invent the car. He was not even the first person to drive a car in Michigan. He was always trying to find better ways to make cars.

In 1896, Henry Ford built his first car. He left his job and started a car company. It was hard going. It took Henry Ford three tries before he got things right. His first two companies failed and went out of business. He started his third company in 1903.

Henry Ford dreamed of making a car that almost anyone could afford. In those days most cars were very expensive. Some cost almost as much as a house! In 1908 Henry got his wish. His new car was called the Model T.

Henry Ford.
Courtesy Michigan
State Archives.

The Model T was a very simple car. If anything went wrong, almost anyone could fix it. It was made in only one color—black. Some people called it the "Tin Lizzie." The car was cheap, but well made. The Model T began to sell well.

The first year over 6,000 were bought. The next year it was over 10,000. Then over 18,000 were sold. Before long over 500,000 Model Ts were sold each year! The Ford company sold more cars than anyone else. Henry Ford's idea was a great success.

Henry Ford made the Model T from 1908 to 1927. Altogether, over fifteen million were sold.

An early Ford assembly line. Courtesy Ford Motor Company.

An Idea Changes Everything

During his life he did many interesting things. He helped start the **moving assembly line** for factories. This was a simple idea, but no one else had put it to use. In those days a group of workers dragged all the parts they needed to a place on the floor. Then they put the parts together to make a car. When they finished the car, it was pushed away and a new one started.

The assembly line carried the car frame along. It went slowly by each worker. Each worker stayed in one place. As the frames moved by, each worker added just one part. Workers became very good at doing their one simple job. Cars were built faster. Costs were cut and more cars were sold.

The moving assembly line changed the way things were done in almost all factories in the world! Working on an assembly line can be boring, but products cost less.

165

Higher Pay Can Save Money!

Henry Ford often did things which surprised people. One year he realized many workers did not stay long at his company. He knew they could not do a good job if they did not have experience.

He had an idea for a way to solve this problem. He decided to pay workers almost double what anyone else paid. The owners of other companies said he was crazy! People stood in long lines to get a job at Ford. The company could choose the very best workers. Years later, Henry Ford said the pay raises saved his company more money than any other idea he ever had!

Henry Ford also hired many African Americans. At that time many companies did not want African American workers. Ford showed them they were wrong.

Henry Ford also built **Greenfield Village** and the **Henry Ford Museum**. He did this so everyone can see what life was like years ago. He wanted people to see real history.

The Dodge Brothers made many cars. This is the first car to have an all steel body. It was made in 1923. Early cars had more wood in them than you might think.
Very special thanks to Bob and Mary Palmer.

Very Important for Michigan & the Country

Since the 1900s, our most important industry has been making cars. Michigan companies sell cars, trucks, and parts all over the world.

The cars were a revolution in transportation. Never before did men and women have so much freedom to go places. They did not need to wait for a train or ship.

But cars and trucks are not much use without good roads. There were few roads when the first cars were sold. Then, most people were content to go a few miles and come home.

What Shall We Drive On?

In 1905, Michigan only had 245 miles of paved roads! Many of the roads were dirt. They were just as they had been for 100 years. Traveling from one city to another was tough. Today Michigan has about 100,000 miles of paved roads. There are almost 2,000 miles of freeways in Michigan.

Early drivers had lots of trouble with bad roads. Only 50 years later, Michigan had some of the best highways in the country.

Courtesy Michigan State Archives

At first, there were few roads because the state was not allowed to build them. The state made a mess when it tried to build railroads and canals in the 1830s. No one wanted to let them try anything else!

Finally, people decided it was time to change those laws. A state highway department was started. Counties began to build more roads too. In 1909 Detroit had the first concrete road in the United States.

In 1916, the national government started to provide money to build highways. Still, it was not until the 1950s that modern highways connected our cities and states.

Today, the state and national governments build and take care of most roads and highways. The counties take care of the rest.

Questions to think about

1. Who started the first car company in Michigan?

2. What was the Model T?

3. Who started the General Motors Company?

4. Who builds and takes care of the roads and highways we use today?

5. Why did Henry Ford pay his workers good wages?

Brain Stretchers
Think about making a product you use. Make a plan for an assembly line to make this product. Use a flow chart if you can.

Words In Action!
The invention of the car changed people's lives. How many changes can you list?

This picture was taken in 1912. Courtesy Michigan State Archives.

Chapter 8   Lesson 1

Two Wars and Other Worries
30 Tough Years

During these years, how did Michigan help in world conflicts?

Why did people need to work so hard to make a living during the 1930s?

World War I Is Coming!

1914 began quietly. Few people noticed the news reports from Europe. Far away countries were talking about war. That was not our problem, was it?

The war in Europe did start. It quickly grew in size. Britain, France, Germany, Russia and others were all fighting.

Michigan was divided. The state had many people whose families came from Germany. Other families came from Britain. It was hard to choose one side or the other.

Should We Help?

The countries at war soon needed more airplanes, **ammunition**, trucks, and ships. Britain and France ordered war supplies from American companies. Many business people welcomed the orders. They hired new workers.

James Couzens was Henry Ford's top executive. Mr. Couzens had British parents. He thought Ford should make supplies for Britain. Mr. Ford did not think so and the men argued.

James Couzens.
Courtesy Michigan
State Archives.

Henry Ford said, "I hate war because war is murder, **desolation**, and **destruction**." He said he would rather burn his factories than make materials for war.

Couzens said, "All right. Then I quit."

"Better think it over, Jim," advised Ford.

"I have. I'm through."

James Couzens left his important job.

Rebecca Shelley tried to stop World War I. Courtesy Bentley Historical Library, University of Michigan. Eleanor Bumgardner Collection.

Stop the Fighting!

Rebecca Shelley, from Battle Creek, was also against the war. Even though she was quite young, she had to do something. She traveled to New York City to speak to the **ambassador** from Germany. The ambassador said, "Yes, all war should be stopped," but that is all he did.

The United States Joins the Fight

The Germans were causing much trouble. A German **submarine** sank a ship with many Americans on board. The Germans seemed to have a plan to help Mexico attack the United States! This was too much.

On April 6, 1917, Congress declared war on Germany. Rebecca Shelley and many others were still against the war. However, Henry Ford had changed his mind. He was now convinced only a show of strength could end the fighting.

Michigan Industry Helps

Michigan workers made many different things for the war effort. They built about 30,000 airplane engines. The Fisher Body plant in Detroit turned out over 2,000 planes. The airplane was a new invention. Less than 1,000 had been made in the entire country before the war.

German submarines sank many ships during World War I. The submarine was a new weapon which terrified people. Art by Aaron Zenz.

Surprisingly, the Ford Motor Company even built 60 ships. These were built at the River Rouge plant and sailed down the river. Many Model T trucks and ambulances went overseas with the U.S. soldiers. Altogether, Detroit made $750 million in supplies for World War I.

In those days, most airplanes were made of fabric and wood. Women in Grand Rapids furniture factories worked on fabric parts for airplanes. Others made plane parts in Bay City.

The War Ends

World War I ended in 1918. Germany surrendered. The United States did much to help Britain and France win. Michigan did its part too.

Michigan women are making parts for wings to go on WWI airplanes. Courtesy Bentley Historical Library, University of Michigan.

171

Our Michigan Adventure

Over 135,000 Michigan men served in the military. Many women also went overseas as nurses. Now, everyone hoped the world would be at peace for a long, long time.

Questions to think about

1. Who was Rebecca Shelley and what did she try to do during World War I?

2. What did Henry Ford say about war? Do you think he was right?

3. Did Michigan do much to help win WWI? Give your reasons.

Brain Stretchers

You are the captain of a small cargo ship in World War I. You must load your ship with airplane parts at Detroit and sail to France. Use a world map and describe your route. Use latitude and longitude. Tell about places you will pass. Remember to watch out for German submarines. Good luck!

Words In Action!

The year is 1916. Write an editorial for your town paper. Tell if the United States should go to war or not.

These soldiers are training at Camp Custer. This was a huge army camp built west of Battle Creek during the war. Courtesy Michigan State Archives.

172

Chapter 8 Lesson 2

Changes After the War

At Last Women Could Vote

Did you know that before 1918 women could not vote in this country? That seems amazing! Several Michigan women worked hard for women's voting rights. In 1918 Michigan's **constitution** was changed so women could vote. Two years later the national laws were changed.

It had been a tough fight for women's voting rights. Men were often against the idea. Some men thought women could not understand election issues.

This tent was at the Michigan state fair grounds. The women were working for the right to vote. What do some of the signs say? Courtesy Michigan State Archives.

One Michigan woman who led in the fight for **equal rights** was **Anna Howard Shaw**.

Her hometown was Big Rapids. The high

These women were working for voting rights while driving across the country. Courtesy Michigan State Archives.

school there has a memorial to Anna. She once said, "Around me I saw women overworked and under-paid... just because they were women..."

A Hero Born in Michigan

In 1927, **Charles Lindbergh** made an exciting first. He was the first person to fly across the Atlantic Ocean alone in a plane. Instantly, Lindbergh was a worldwide hero. People in Detroit were proud because Lindbergh was born there. Also his mother was a science teacher in Detroit .

Charles Lindbergh. He was the first person to fly across the Atlantic Ocean alone. Courtesy Michigan State Archives.

Sound from a Box

In the 1920s and 1930s people were thrilled by a new invention, the radio. In 1930, station WXYZ began in Detroit.

Michigan radio station WWJ in 1931. The announcer is at the left. The other people are making sound effects for the program. Courtesy Michigan State Archives.

The staff was talking over ideas for a new program. They thought about a story with a hero from the wild west. The **Lone Ranger** was created! From 1932 until 1954, live radio stories about the masked man were sent across the nation *from Detroit*!

Questions to think about

1. When was the first year Michigan women were able to vote?

2. Name two core democratic values kept from women before they could vote. (List on page 251)

3. Name a Michiganian who worked to allow women to vote.

4. How is Charles Lindbergh connected to Michigan?

5. What does the Lone Ranger have to do with Michigan?

Brain Stretchers
Early radio programs used many things to make sound effects. Think of five things you can use to make different sounds for a radio program.

Words In Action!
Pretend you have a great, great grandmother who voted for the first time in 1918. Interview her about voting for the first time. What did she think about it? What did the men think about it?

Core- the most important part of anything-
like the core of an apple

Democratic- the kind of government
run by the people with freedom for all

Values- important beliefs that guide your life

Chapter 8 Lesson 3

The Good Times End

Once World War I ended, people felt very good. They were glad there was peace at last. They spent money and bought things they had waited to buy. More cars were sold each year. Business became better and better.

The **stock market** had gone up and up. Millions of people had bought stocks even though the prices were higher than ever before. Investors thought stocks would go up forever. But in October 1929, they suddenly went down! People said it was a **stock market crash**. Everyone wanted to sell their stocks, but no one wanted to buy. Stock prices went lower and lower.

In 1929 the stock market crashed. Many people thought they were rich one day but had no money the next! Art by Aaron Zenz.

Banks Close- Savings Lost

The stock market crash also hurt banks. Many of them invested in stocks too. Often banks had to close. By 1932 nearly 200 Michigan banks had gone out of business. Many people lost all of their savings- savings they would need because they had also lost their jobs!

Less Business - Fewer Jobs

Now people simply did not have money to buy things. Business sales fell rapidly. Michigan business was tied closely to car sales. In Genesee county, half of the working people had jobs with General Motors.

There were almost 4.5 million cars sold in the country in 1929. The next year there were less than 3 million sold. The year after that, sales fell to less than 2 million.

As a result, many workers lost their jobs. The Ford Rouge plant had 98,337 workers in 1929. By 1933 there were only 28,915! In Lansing only one-third of the workers who had jobs in 1929 still worked in 1930.

Business was so bad, the years after 1929 were called **The Great Depression**! This slowdown lasted nearly 10 years.

What Could be Done?

In 1932, the federal government started programs to help the jobless. One was called the **WPA.** It hired artists, carpenters, and writers who were out of work. They painted pictures in post offices and other buildings. They built roadside park buildings and wrote articles. In 1938, Michigan had over 200,000 people in WPA jobs.

There was another program which helped Michigan. This was the **CCC**. The CCC was for young men. The men in the CCC lived in big camps much like the army. Actually, army officers were in charge. They kept strict

CCC men at lunch break in the 1930s. Courtesy Michigan State Archives

rules. The members of the CCC had a clean place to sleep, hot meals, clothes, and educational programs. Men in the CCC fought forest fires, built trails, roads, campgrounds, parks, and planted trees.

Joe Louis- World Boxing Champion-1937

Joe Louis came with his family to Michigan in 1926. He was 12 at the time. His teenage years were spent in Detroit. He was a big, strong young man. It was in Detroit that he learned to box.

In 1937, Joe Louis won the world's heavyweight boxing championship. He defeated a German boxer backed by the **Nazi** government. Joe successfully defended his title 25 times between 1937 and 1948.

In 1978 Detroit named its new sports arena in his honor. It was said "Joe had *more* than fighting greatness. He was great as a man."

Questions To Think About

1. What was the big business slowdown called which began in 1929?

2. Give one example of a project done by the WPA and one by the CCC.

3. Who was Joe Louis and what did he do?

4. Name three ways the Great Depression changed life in Michigan.

Brain Stretchers
Make a chart or graph which shows how much Michigan business went down in the Great Depression.

Words In Action!
Write four questions you would like to ask someone from this lesson if you could interview them.

Write a short story telling what life might have been like in Michigan during the Great Depression years.

Heavyweight boxing champion Joe Louis talking to children.
Courtesy Michigan State Archives.

Chapter 8 Lesson 4
Workers Need Help!

The hard work and fast speed of the assembly line upset many workers. Do you think this factory is well heated? In the 1930s they started unions to try to have better conditions in the factories. Courtesy Michigan State Archives.

Many people did not have jobs in the 1930s. For those who did have jobs, life was still not easy. Sales were way down. Companies had to cut costs or go out of business. The companies pushed their workers to do more for less pay. If a worker complained, he or she could be replaced in a minute!

This is what one worker on a car assembly line said: "I was only 15 feet away from a drinking fountain, but the line went by so fast I could never get enough ahead with my work to run over and get a quick drink!"

Another worker ground off the rough edges of car bodies. In 1928 he did eight bodies a day. He was paid $1.00 an hour for his work. By 1932 he did 32 car bodies a day and was paid 35 cents an hour!

Who Can Help Us?

Workers began to think **labor unions** could help them with their problems. Unions are groups of workers formed to get better working conditions and wages. They try to make a deal with the company for all the workers. This is called **bargaining**. If a good deal cannot be made, the workers will stop working. This is known as a **strike.**

Walter Reuther

Walter Reuther moved to Michigan in 1927 so he could earn more money. He found a job at the Ford Motor Company.

Mr. Reuther became involved in union activities. He and his two brothers became union leaders. His family always believed in trying to help people. They worked to help the **United Auto Workers** union grow. This union was also called the **UAW**.

Walter Reuther helped start the United Auto Workers union. Art by Aaron Zenz.

Unions Not Always Popular

Few companies would accept the idea of a union. They did not want their workers to belong to them. The companies felt the unions were telling them how to run their businesses.

The companies certainly did not like strikes. A strike meant no cars would be finished. A strike was also hard for the union members. They would have no pay during the strike. Still, conditions in the car plants were getting worse.

The 1937 sit-down strike at General Motors. Courtesy Michigan State Archives.

The Great Sit-Down Strike

A major strike took place at the General Motors Fisher Body plants in **Flint**. Suddenly on December 30, 1936, workers stopped and sat down in the plant. They wouldn't leave to go home. It was a **sit-down** strike. They blocked the doors so machines and parts could not be taken out. The workers

181

said they were tired of low wages, poor working conditions, and little **job security**.

General Motors wanted the factories going again. They urged the police to go after the strikers. On January 11, 1937 the police fired tear gas into the Fisher Body plant #2. The workers would not budge. Everyone was very tense. What would happen next?

The Governor Comes

Governor **Frank Murphy** came to Flint to calm things down. He ordered 3,000 National Guard soldiers to Flint too. They arrived with all their battle gear. Days of arguing took place!

Victory For the Union

On February 11,1937, after 44 days, General Motors said the company would give in. The United Auto Workers won the right to represent GM workers. Wages were increased. The strikers were joyous and the city of Flint breathed a sigh of relief.

Governor Frank Murphy. Courtesy Michigan State Archives.

In 1939, the courts ruled that sit-down strikes were not legal. If workers want to strike, they must be outside the factory.

There are strong unions in Michigan today. In many ways unions have helped workers. Pay has gone up. Working hours are better. Of course these things also mean products can cost more. Sometimes companies

move their factories to places which do not have strong unions. This can mean fewer jobs in Michigan.

Questions to think about

1. Give some reasons workers wanted to join unions in the 1930s.

2. Was Walter Reuther for or against unions?

3. Where and when was there a famous sit-down strike?

4. Explain what a strike is.

5. What does UAW stand for?

Brain Stretchers

Do you think the U.A.W. union was working toward the core democratic value called the "common good" during the 1930s? Explain your opinion in a paragraph.

In 1935 a can of peaches or a movie cost 10¢. A worker with a "good" job making cars might earn 35¢ an hour. Make a chart comparing those three things in 1935 and another comparing them today. You will need to find out the costs today and the wages today.

Words In Action!

Your thoughts about unions may depend on who you are and which job you have. It is the 1930s. Take your choice- be a union leader or an owner of an auto company. Write a letter to the editor of your newspaper. Give your views on the situation in your car factory.

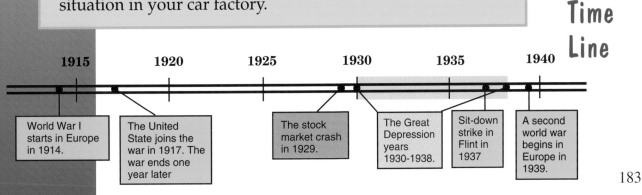

Time Line

| 1915 | 1920 | 1925 | 1930 | 1935 | 1940 |

World War I starts in Europe in 1914.

The United State joins the war in 1917. The war ends one year later

The stock market crash in 1929.

The Great Depression years 1930-1938.

Sit-down strike in Flint in 1937

A second world war begins in Europe in 1939.

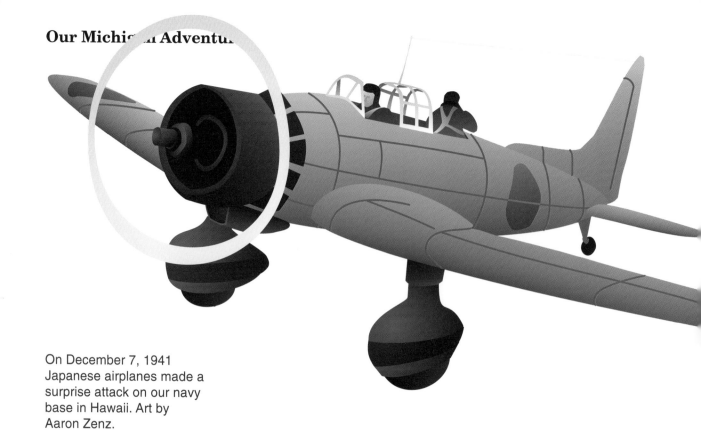

On December 7, 1941 Japanese airplanes made a surprise attack on our navy base in Hawaii. Art by Aaron Zenz.

Chapter 8 Lesson 5

World War II

The bad days of the Great Depression began to fade away. In 1940 more people had jobs. They were spending more money. Life was looking better.

Then war started in Europe and China. Germany invaded Poland and France. Japan attacked China. That was certainly a concern, but more jobs and more money helped people feel better. They did not worry too much about the United States joining the war.

Surprise Attack!

On Sunday, December 7, 1941, America was jolted. The Japanese sent 432 planes to bomb our navy at **Pearl Harbor**. Pearl Harbor is in the Hawaiian Islands.

Chapter 8 *Two Wars and Other Worries*

Michigan sailors like Jim Green were there. He was lucky. He survived the attack even though he was in gun turret No. 4 of the battleship *Arizona*. The *Arizona* sank when a bomb hit its ammunition storage. Sadly, 1,177 of Jim's shipmates lost their lives. Much of our navy was destroyed. We had no choice. The United States had to go to war!

A Second Big War

Germany and Japan had now attacked the nations which stood for freedom. There was fighting in Europe, the Pacific Ocean region, and Asia. World War II was now in full swing.

The Soo Locks in the Upper Peninsula were a very important transportation link. That area became heavily guarded. Searchlights and radar scanned the sky for enemy planes. Everyone was afraid of an attack there.

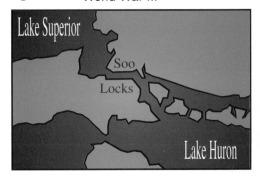

The Soo Locks were carefully guarded during World War II.

This World War II tank was made in Michigan. Courtesy Michigan State Archives.

Switching from Cars to Tanks

There was a rush to reorganize factories. They would be making airplanes and tanks now. New machines were installed. Some of the old machines were put into storage. The assembly lines were adjusted to carry different parts.

Michigan's factories made all kinds of military supplies. So much was made in Michigan, our state earned the title, **Arsenal of Democracy.**

This Lansing woman is checking cannon shells during World War II. Courtesy Michigan State Archives.

This is the huge Willow Run bomber plant. It made B-24 bombers. Courtesy Michigan State Archives.

Michigan Factories A Big Help

The shipyards in Bay City made ships for the navy. In Midland, Dow Chemical made lightweight metal for airplanes. Kelloggs of Battle Creek made food for soldiers.

Saginaw Steering Gear made over 300,000 machine guns. In Kalamazoo, the Upjohn company made medicine for soldiers wounded in battle. The Packard company made engines for the navy's PT boats.

The Ford company built a very large factory to make B-24 bombers. The factory was called **Willow Run** and it was built near Ypsilanti. At one time, 42,000 people worked there. Many of those workers were women. About 8,000 bombers were built at Willow Run.

The Upper Peninsula increased output of its valuable copper and iron ore too. The Ford company made over 4,000 glider planes in Iron Mountain.

Chapter 8 *Two Wars and Other Worries*

You Can Help Too!

Thousands of school children gathered milkweed pods. These went into life jackets which were made in Petoskey.

Farmers grew more food than ever before. That wasn't easy with so many farm workers away fighting. People who were too old or too young to fight helped on the farms.

This group of men is leaving Detroit to join the military in World War II. Courtesy Michigan State Archives.

Everyone Works or Fights

Men and women rushed to join the army, navy, marines, and the air force. They all wanted to help their country. During the war, over 600,000 Michigan men and women joined the military.

The military began to use women and African Americans more and more. Some Michigan women helped to fly airplanes from the factories to the air bases. Faye Wolf of Grand Rapids was one of those women. Some women were killed in training accidents. Other women pilots crashed because their planes had engine problems.

Problems on the Home Front

Working during the war was not easy. All kinds of things were soon hard to find. The government began to **ration** food, gasoline, tires, and many other items. A ration meant each family could only have a certain amount. People could only buy four gallons of gasoline each week. To save gas, the govern-

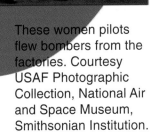

These women pilots flew bombers from the factories. Courtesy USAF Photographic Collection, National Air and Space Museum, Smithsonian Institution.

187

This is a book of ration coupons from World War II. If you had used all of your coupons, you could not buy more of the items. Courtesy Stella McConnell.

ment set the speed limit at 35 miles an hour! People could only buy so many pounds of sugar or meat each month.

Peace Returns

World War II ended in 1945. Germany and then Japan surrendered. The men and women in the army, navy, marines, and air force began to come home.

The first new car in three years rolled off the assembly line. People were eager to buy all of the things they couldn't during the war. The demand for new cars was tremendous. It was the beginning of a long boom in Michigan's economy.

Questions to think about

1. During World War II, which place in Michigan did people think might be attacked?

2. What was the nickname given to Michigan during World War II? What was the reason for the nickname?

3. What war work was done at Willow Run?

Brain Stretchers
During World War II, which core democratic values from page 251 were U.S. soldiers helping defend? List them.

Words In Action!
Use facts from this lesson to help make a story about living in Michigan during World War II.

Write a simple plan to change your factory from making cars to tanks for World War II.

Chapter 9   Lesson 1

Michigan to the Year 2000 & Beyond

What event has changed our state the most in the last 50 years?

What Is In the News- the 1950s

After the war, thousands of young men and women came back from the military. They wanted to buy new homes. They wanted new cars. They needed jobs.

New homes were built in the **suburbs.** A suburb is a smaller town at the edge of a larger city. Then came shopping malls and interstate highways. The government was building many interstate highways in the 1950s.

Before the Mackinac Bridge was built, many cars often waited to cross the Straits of Mackinac. Courtesy Michigan State Archives.

Mackinac Bridge- Connecting the Peninsulas

The new highways were great, but all cars and trucks had to stop at the Straits of Mackinac. There was no way to drive from one side to the other. Nearly five miles of water separate the peninsulas.

A bridge was needed, but it would be such a long bridge. Could it ever be built? Would the rock under the water hold up the bridge? Would a storm blow it down? How would the costs be paid?

Ferry boats carried cars across the Straits of Mackinac. Wasn't that good enough? Well, there were often long lines waiting for the boats. At times it could take a day for drivers to go across!

The Mackinac Bridge. Courtesy of Travel Michigan.

Dr. David Steinman designed the Mackinac Bridge. He is on the bridge while it is being built. Courtesy Mackinac Bridge Authority and the Michigan Department of Transportation.

Bridge Ideas Take Shape

Could the state government borrow the money to build the bridge? Would the fares charged to cross it pay the interest on the borrowed money? People were trying to answer those questions.

Dr. David Steinman (STINE man) was an expert in designing bridges. He designed a bridge to cross the Straits. He said it could be done. The bridge would be safe and strong.

Finally, state government decided to go ahead. Over 2,000 construction workers moved to the Straits. The huge project began in 1954.

Much of the work was quite dangerous. The builders worked while hanging from two main cables high above the water. During the time the bridge was being built, five workers were killed in accidents.

Opening day finally arrived. The first cars used the Mackinac Bridge on November 1, 1957. Now Michigan's two peninsulas were connected!

Each year nearly 2 million cars and trucks cross the bridge! The bridge has made it much easier for people and products to reach one peninsula from the other. It is another important Michigan transportation link.

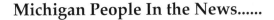

Michigan People In the News......

Dewey for President

The 1948 Presidential election was a close one. Michigan had a special interest in the result. The Republican **nominee** was **Thomas E. Dewey**. Dewey grew up in **Owosso**, Michigan. Almost everyone thought Dewey would beat President Harry Truman. However, President Truman had a surprise victory and was re-elected.

Thomas Dewey from Owosso, Michigan. He ran for President, but lost. Art by Aaron Zenz.

A Nobel Prize Winner

After the war, the country of Israel was being formed. This was a big event in the news. Unfortunately, there were many problems between Arab and Jewish people in starting the new country. There was fighting and arguing. The new United Nations (UN) worked to settle the situation.

Ralph Bunche. Courtesy Bentley Historical Library, University of Michigan. James Kerr Pollock Collection.

Ralph Bunche was born in Detroit. He became a member of the UN team sent to that area. This was not an easy or safe job. In 1948, one of his teammates was killed. Then Mr. Bunche became the leading **negotiator**.

For his work with that problem, he was awarded the **Nobel Peace Prize** in 1950. Bunche was the first African American to receive that award.

191

Civil Rights!

Equality and justice are two core democratic values civil rights workers fought to have.

Struggling for Civil Rights

During the 1960s minorities worked hard for their **civil rights.** Civil rights are the right to fair and equal treatment without considering a person's color, race, or religion.

Different African American people had different ideas about how to change things. Many felt peaceful protests were the best way. Others, like **Malcolm X**, believed that anything should be used to force changes. Malcolm X grew up in Lansing, Michigan.

Malcolm X. Courtesy Michigan State Archives.

Dr. Martin Luther King was a leader who believed in peace. In 1963, Dr. King led a civil rights march in Detroit. He joined 125,000 people who walked down Woodward Avenue. He said, "Now is the time to lift our nation from the quicksands of **racial injustice**.... Now is the time to get rid of **segregation** and **discrimination**."

Dr. Martin Luther King during the 1963 Detroit march. Courtesy Michigan State Archives.

Chapter 9 *Michigan to the Year 2000 & Beyond*

Success from Songs

Detroit was the birthplace of **Motown** Industries. Motown became one of the most successful African American businesses in the United States. **Berry Gordy** started Motown as a record company. That was in 1959. **Smokey Robinson**'s 1960 record, "Shop Around" was one of the first great hits! Motown soon had sales of $50 million a year.

The **Supremes** and **Stevie Wonder** also recorded for Motown. Stevie Wonder was born blind. When he was just nine years old he spent hours visiting the Motown studios. He played every instrument he could find. He was called the "little boy wonder."

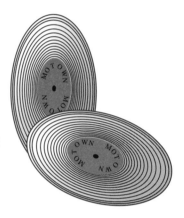

Questions to think about

1. Name the man born in Owosso who ran for President in 1948. Did he win?

2. Who was the first African American to win a Nobel Peace Prize?

3. Who designed the Mackinac Bridge? When did the bridge open?

4. Who started the Motown Record Company? Name two musicians or groups who recorded with Motown.

Brain Stretchers

Imagine you are on Dr. Steinman's staff. You must plan the stages for building the Mackinac Bridge. What will you do first, second, third, and so forth.

Words In Action!

Write words to your own song about Michigan!

Chapter 9 Lesson 2

Want to Take Their Places?

Meet some modern day explorers. What they do today is somewhat like the early French explorers of long ago. The French were exploring the earth. These are astronauts who are exploring outer space. No spaceships were launched from Michigan. Still, several Michigan people have been a part of the space program.

Roger Chaffee from Grand Rapids was one of the first. In 1967 he was one of three astronauts in a test launch when the space capsule suddenly caught fire. Before anyone could help the astronauts, they were killed by the flames! **Jack Lousma** was another astronaut from Grand Rapids. During 1973 he spent two months aboard Skylab.

James McDivitt from Jackson piloted the spacecraft for the first space walk. Al Worden, also from Jackson, commanded the 1971 Apollo 15 flight to the moon. The city of Jackson has a space museum to honor their astronauts.

Brewster Shaw is from Cass City in the "thumb" area. Shaw flew in the space shuttle *Columbia* in 1983 and commanded the shuttle *Atlantis* in 1985.

Jerry Linenger is from Eastpointe, Michigan. During 1997 he spent *five months* aboard the Russian Mir Space Station! His work on Mir is a joint project between Russia and the United States.

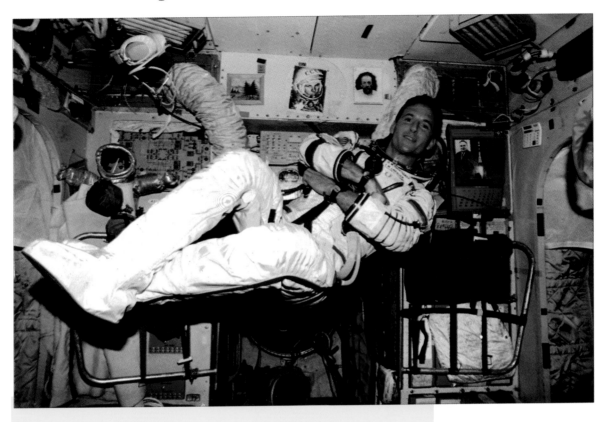

Before Jerry left, he was asked what he would miss most about being away. He said it would be hard being away from his son for so long.

Astronaut Jerry Linenger aboard the Mir space station. Courtesy of NASA.

During those five months, Jerry e-mailed letters to his son. Those letters were shared on the Internet by NASA. Each letter was about a different topic. A few of Jerry's e-mails are about:

Early explorers never talked to their loved ones
Up here, you either make it, bring it, or do without it
We all depend on each other
Space is an unforgiving place

Jerry Linenger compares his space travel to an adventure. Perhaps some day it will become the place we will call home!

A President From Michigan

Gerald Ford became the 38th President of the United States on August 9, 1974. Before that, he was Vice President for a short time. Earlier, Gerald Ford represented the Grand Rapids area in Congress for 25 years.

Michigan has had many famous people, but Gerald Ford is the only person to ever be President. You can learn all about President Ford at Gerald Ford Museum in Grand Rapids.

President Gerald Ford. Courtesy Gerald R. Ford Presidential Library.

Former Detroit Tiger Alan Trammell - one of the all time greats. Courtesy of Joe Arcure Detroit Tigers photographer.

Michigan Sports Greats

Look at that baseball go. What a hit! Michiganians have cheered the Tigers for years. Ty Cobb began playing with the Tigers in 1905. He was the first player named to the National Baseball Hall of Fame. There have been many other famous Tigers over the years like Hank Greenburg, Denny McLain, and Al Kaline. How many others can you name?

Minor Leagues

Some cities have added minor league baseball teams. Lansing's Lugnuts are one example. The city of Lansing has built an exciting downtown stadium for the Lugnuts. It is Oldsmobile Park. Grand Rapids has the Whitecaps playing at Old Kent Park. Fans in Battle Creek watch the Battle Cats and those in Kalamazoo see the Kodiaks.

Comerica Park where the Detroit Tigers play. Courtesy of the author.

Ice Hockey

Hockey is a favorite sport for many people. They love to see the puck sizzle over the ice and into the net. And the puck does sizzle when the Detroit Red Wings play in the Stanley Cup games.

Years ago one of their outstanding Redwings was Gordie Howe. Gordie Howe holds many records. Today the Redwings have Sergei Fedorov and Steve Yzerman.

The Detroit Red Wings. Courtesy of John Hartman and the Detroit Red Wings.

Basketball

"Smoking sneakers," we can't forget Earvin "Magic" Johnson! Basketball lovers from mid-Michigan enjoyed his playing for many years. Lansing is Magic Johnson's hometown. He played basketball for Michigan State University. He helped that team win the N.C.A.A. title. He also played with the Los Angeles Lakers. He helped them win five NBA titles!

Football

Each fall many sports fans put on their coats and head to the football stadiums. They hold their breaths waiting for that last touchdown. The great college teams or the Detroit Lions can offer an exciting game.

The Olympics

Some of the state's great athletes are always looking toward the next Olympic Games. Sheila Young-Ochowicz was an Olympic speed skating champion in

1976. Not every athlete wins a medal. Hillsdale's Penny Neer-Thayer competed in the 1992 Olympic discus events. Besides the regular Olympics, there is a Senior Olympics for older athletes. Robert McConnell of Hillsdale competed in the 1997 U.S. Senior Olympics with his 100 meter backstroke.

Questions to think about

1. Which astronaut with ties to Michigan has been in space on the longest mission?

2. Who was the 38th President of the United States? What did he have to do with Michigan?

3. Which city is Earvin "Magic" Johnson's hometown?

4. Choose four events mentioned in this chapter and make a time line using them.

Brain Stretchers
Make an acrostic using the names of people in this chapter. Have the acrostic spell MICHIGAN.

Words In Action!
Use the internet to find information about a person or event from this chapter. Keep notes on how you found the sites you visited. List the sites and tell what you learned at each site.

Chapter 10 Lesson 1

Neat Stuff We Make and Grow

How can Michigan produce and grow so many products?

Dodge Dakota pick-up trucks being made at the Warren Truck Assembly Plant in Warren, Courtesy Daimler-Chrysler Corporation.

Sharing Facts About Michigan Products

Suppose your class decides to be e-mail pals with a class far away. Your teacher finds a fourth grade class in a Florida school. Everyone in your class is really excited. You decide you want your new Florida friends to know more about Michigan!

You read to find out more about the things made and grown here. Soon you are really surprised. You had no idea so many things we see each day are made here- right in Michigan!

This picture shows cars being welded by robotic welders. © General Motors Corporation. GM Media Archives.

Cars and Trucks

You learn two American car companies have their **headquarters** in Michigan. Several have factories here. Daimler-Chrysler, Ford, and General Motors are the largest. General Motors is one of the biggest companies of any kind in the world!

Nearly half of all factory jobs in Michigan involve making **motor vehicles** and parts! About 290,000 of our people work for the three biggest car companies. General Motors has the most workers.

When Will Kellogg was a young man he tried several jobs. Once he sold brooms. It took years before he succeeded in the breakfast cereal business. Art by Aaron Zenz.

Many medicines are made in Kalamazoo. These workers are packaging some at the Pharmacia & Upjohn company. Courtesy Pharmacia & Upjohn Inc.

Breakfast Cereal

Then there is breakfast cereal. People all over the world eat breakfast cereal. Kellogg, Post and Ralston cereals are made in Battle Creek. Battle Creek is known as the home of breakfast cereals.

Dr. Harvey Kellogg and his brother **Will Kellogg** invented some of those first cereals. Will Kellogg began selling cereal in 1906. His first cereal was toasted corn flakes.

A corn flakes packing line at Kellogg's Courtesy Kellogg Company, Inc.

Other Foods

Other delicious foods are made in Michigan too. The Bob Evans company makes sausage and other foods in Hillsdale. Hillsdale also has a large plant making flour for doughnuts. The Jiffy mixes you see in many grocery stores are made in Chelsea. When you were a baby, you probably ate Gerber's baby food which is made in Fremont.

Medicine and Vitamins

Some of you may take a vitamin at breakfast. Several kinds of medicine and vitamins are made in Kalamazoo. These are made by the Pharmacia & Upjohn Company.

Dr. William Upjohn was a family doctor in the horse and buggy days. He began making pills when some of those he bought would not dissolve.

The company Dr. Upjohn started has really grown over the years. In 1995 it merged with a Swedish company. It has many scientists who spend their time looking for new medicines.

Questions to think about

1. Which motor vehicle maker has the most workers?

2. About when did the breakfast cereal business start? Name two Michigan cereal makers.

3. List six Michigan businesses and the city associated with each one.

Tugboats, Barges -Ontonagon

Ceiling Tiles -L'Anse

Paper -Munising

Snowshoes -Shingleton

Paper -Escanaba

Michigan Made!

Cutting Blocks -Petoskey

Log Cabins -Boyne Falls

Cement, Wood Products -Alpena

Frozen Foods -Traverse City

Plastic Wrap, Chemicals -Midland

Pleasure Boats -Cadillac

Boats, Cranes, Potato Chips -Bay City

Baby Food -Fremont

Shoes -Rockford

Car Parts, Sugar -Saginaw

Spark Plugs, Car Bodies -Flint

Office Furniture, Tank Engines -Muskegon

Cars -Lansing

Paper -Port Huron

Cars -Pontiac

Chalkboards, Wooden Shoes -Holland

Office Furniture, Household Goods -Grand Rapids

Solar Cells -Troy

Trucks, Tanks -Warren

Cars, Car Parts, Candy -Detroit

Washers & Driers -Benton Harbor

Peanut Butter -Livonia

Electronics -St. Joseph

Scientific Equipment, Printing -Ann Arbor

Robots, Medicine, Mint Oil -Kalamazoo

Cereals -Battle Creek

Baking Mixes -Chelsea

Magic Supplies -Colon

Doughnut Flour -Hillsdale

This is a well which brings salt water or brine to the surface. It is near the Dow Chemical plant in Midland, Michigan.

Below is a bubble of Saran Wrap. Saran Wrap was first sold in stores in 1952. It was developed in Midland. Courtesy Dow Chemical Company.

Chapter 10 Lesson 2

Using Nature for More Products

About the time Dr. Upjohn was thinking about ways to make pills, another man came to Michigan. He was Herbert Dow. Mr. Dow knew that Michigan had much salt and salt water under it. The salt was left by a huge ocean which once covered the state.

Some people had wells to bring the saltwater to the surface. This salty water is called **brine**. Herbert Dow knew a lot about science. He tested the brine and found other chemicals too. He wondered what he could make with them. He invented a clever way to take one of those chemicals out of the brine.

Herbert Dow began the Dow Chemical Company in Midland, Michigan. Mr. Dow started his business here because Michigan has so much brine. This was in 1897. Soon his company was making many chemicals from brine. Now Dow is the second largest chemical company in the country.

About the time of World War II, some Dow scientists were experimenting with plastics. They made a clear, tough, plastic wrap. **Saran Wrap** was born!

For many years Saran Wrap was made in Midland. It is an interesting process. The plastic is melted and blown into big bubbles. The bubbles are rolled up and cut into strips. Those strips go into the boxes people buy.

Businesses often begin near the **raw materials** they use. Dow Chemical is near the brine it uses. Michigan iron ore is made into steel for cars. Michigan corn goes into corn flakes. Wood was used to make furniture in Grand Rapids.

Furniture From West Michigan

At first the furniture makers were small. In the late 1800s they began to **advertise.** They made photographs of their furniture. They sent the photographs all over the country. They sold more and more furniture. Railroads took the furniture to customers in many states. Grand Rapids became the furniture capital of the entire country.

After many years, the furniture business changed. Furniture makers found it was cheaper to make wooden furniture elsewhere. The Grand Rapids factories began to close, but some of them did not give up. They began to make more furniture for offices and schools.

This picture shows some of the modern office furniture made at the Herman Miller Company in Zeeland, Michigan. Courtesy Herman Miller, Inc.

Clockwise from left:

Steelcase headquarters building.

The factory at Steelcase.

Checking and testing is important in making high quality products.

A worker is grinding furniture parts at Steelcase.

All photos courtesy of the Steelcase Corporation.

203

Now Grand Rapids and the nearby cities are known for making office furniture. Companies like Steelcase and Herman Miller sell billions of dollars worth each year. Many people in western Michigan make office furniture. Some of it is even shipped to other countries like Mexico.

Products to Stand On!

You can ride in Michigan cars. You can eat Michigan food products. You can sit on Michigan furniture. You can even stand in a Michigan product- shoes!

The Wolverine World Wide company makes Hush Puppy shoes in Rockford, Michigan. This company has one of the world's largest leather making factories.

While you have on your Michigan shoes, you might be on another Michigan product. The sidewalk you walk on could be made from Michigan cement. Yes, cement is made in Michigan! Alpena has one of the world's largest cement plants.

Ships bring the limestone to Alpena to make the cement. Some of that limestone comes from Rogers City.

Magic Is Big Business

When it is time for some fun, go to Colon, Michigan. Colon has the world's largest maker of magic supplies and tricks. Maybe you can figure out how magicians pull rabbits out of the hat!

Many things for magic tricks are made in Colon, Michigan. Art by Theresa Deeter.

Thinking About Christmas?

As Christmas comes near, some of you may think about model trains. The Lionel company makes toy trains in its factory near Mt. Clemens. The Kalamazoo Toy Train Company makes them in Bangor.

While you are making out your Christmas list, don't forget decorations for the tree. There is no better place to buy these than Bronner's huge store in Frankenmuth. Bronner's specializes in Christmas decorations.

Who Is the Largest?

Michigan has many companies known around the world. Some Michigan companies are really huge. They may have hundreds of thousands of workers! General Motors and Ford are two of the largest companies in the world.

Here is a list of some of the largest companies with headquarters in Michigan. They may also have factories and offices in other places.

Which Michigan Companies Sell the Most

General Motors	$164 billion
Ford Motor	$147 billion
Chrysler	$61 billion
Dow Chemical	$20 billion
Whirlpool	$8.5 billion
Pharmacia & Upjohn	$7.2 billion
Amway	$6.8 billion
Kellogg	$6.6 billion
Domino's Pizza	$2.5 billion

These numbers are for a recent year. The numbers will change from year to year and the order may change too. (*Source: Michigan Statistical Abstract*)

Thomas Monaghan, the founder of Domino's Pizza. The Domino's headquarters is in Ann Arbor, Michigan.

So many products are made here, it is hard to list all of them. Do you know about any made in your home town? Just remember, Michigan has products you can sit in, stand on, wear, eat, ride, and play with!

Imports and Exports

Michigan has some great products and great companies. Things made here are wanted all over the world. Many of Michigan's companies sell their products in other countries.

The Canadian flag

the Japanese flag

Where Michigan Products Go	
Canada	$11.5 billion
Mexico	$5.6 billion
Japan	$1.1 billion
Saudi Arabia	$0.98 billion
Germany	$0.91 billion

When we sell things to other countries, they are called **exports**. It is good we can export products. This brings money to Michigan. It makes jobs for Michigan people.

Buying From Other Countries- Imports

However, we cannot make everything here. Often we need to buy products from other countries. When we buy a product from another country, it is called an **import**.

Most of Our Imports Are From These Countries

Canada (sends the most)
Japan
Germany
Britain (United Kingdom)
France
China
Italy (sends the least of these countries)

the French flag

Questions to think about

1. Why is the Dow company located in Midland?

2. Much office furniture is made near this city. Name it.

3. How does Great Lakes shipping help the cement business in Alpena?

4. Which Michigan product do you think is the most interesting? Tell why you think it is interesting. Tell what you have learned about it.

5. What is the difference between an export and an import?

6. Name two countries which do much importing and exporting with Michigan.

Brain Stretchers
Choose three Michigan companies from this lesson. Make a chart to show how much they sell each year. Use pictures of their products as a part of your chart.

Words In Action!
Choose a Michigan product and write an ad for this product. Explain why people should buy it. Tell how much it costs and other important facts.

Have you visited a Michigan company to watch how the product is made? Write about your visit and tell what you saw.

Chapter 10 Lesson 3

Good Things to Eat From Michigan

Maybe we should call Michigan the yummy state! All kinds of good food are produced here. Fruit, vegetables, meat and dairy foods are all from our state.

Certain parts of Michigan have just the right growing conditions for some foods. The climate and soil make Michigan the leader for several crops.

Michigan Fruit

We have lots of cherries. They come from Traverse City and other towns near Lake Michigan. The water of the lake helps to make the weather just right. Fruit grows very well along the western edge of the Lower Peninsula. This area is called the **fruit belt.**

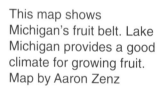

This map shows Michigan's fruit belt. Lake Michigan provides a good climate for growing fruit. Map by Aaron Zenz

Michigan grows more tart cherries than any other state. Traverse City is in the heart of the cherry growing region. Art by David McConnell.

Michigan is the biggest producer of **tart cherries** in the United States. If all our cherries went into just one pie, it would be a monster. It would weigh more than 250 million pounds!

Michigan also grows more blueberries than any other state.

Michigan is the second largest apple growing state in the country. Courtesy Michigan Apple Committee.

Apples and peaches are grown in several parts of Michigan. Apples grow well where there is a cold winter and warm summer. Michigan is second in the country for growing apples. Our farmers grow about one billion pounds of apples each year!

Beans, Beans, Beans

Ready for some hot chili with plenty of beans? Michigan grows about 600 million pounds of beans each year! We grow more dry beans than any other state. Dry beans are kinds other than green beans. Michigan grows almost one-fifth of the entire world's supply!

These beans are grown around Saginaw and Bay City. So many beans are grown that we cannot eat them all. What happens to the rest? They are exported to Europe on ships. Look at the picture to see all the kinds of Michigan dry beans.

Michigan grows cranberry beans, white beans, navy beans, black turtle beans, and yellow eye beans

Something Sweet

Nearby is the **thumb** of the Lower Peninsula. Farmers in the thumb area grow an unusual crop- **sugar beets.** These beets are not eaten in the way you may think they would be. They are used to make sugar. The sugar from these beets is just like the sugar from sugar cane. The sugar you buy in the store could be from Michigan sugar beets.

A Michigan sugar beet. It is hard to believe something sweet can come from this! Courtesy David McConnell.

The maple syrup you use on pancakes or waffles may come from Michigan. Michigan is one of the leading makers of maple syrup.

Green Sprouts

Much celery is grown here too. The farmers around Kalamazoo were pioneers in growing celery in this country. Long ago, Michigan was the number one grower of celery. Now more celery comes from California. Today we are the third biggest celery grower.

If you drive around Kalamazoo county, you may see another large business which grows things. The plants grown by this business are not eaten. This is the bedding plant business. Bedding plants are started here and then shipped to other green houses. Easter lilies and hanging flower baskets are also grown in Michigan. Tulip bulbs are grown near Holland.

The growing of celery as a vegetable began near Kalamazoo. Courtesy David McConnell.

Moo!

Don't forget Michigan cattle. They give us beef and milk. The dairy business brings Michigan farmers the most money of all. Producing milk brings more money than any other Michigan farm business.

Value of Michigan Food Products for a Recent Year

12 million dollars	Grapes
14 million dollars	Celery
35 million dollars	Tart Cherries
85 million dollars	Apples
115 million dollars	Sugar
120 million dollars	Dry Beans
180 million dollars	Pork (pigs)
260 million dollars	Beef
315 million dollars	Soybeans
560 million dollars	Corn
745 million dollars	Milk

Top: Registered Holstein cows on the Michael and Susan Dietz dairy farm. Courtesy Michael and Susan Dietz.

Bottom: Veterinarian Dr. Dean Gibbons checks a calf with pneumonia. Courtesy Michael and Susan Dietz.

How Much We Grow Each Year
Millions of Pounds (Yes- millions!)

Apples	1,000	Cucumber	350
Beans (dry)	600	Grapes	98
Beef	485	Milk	5,400
Celery	113	Pork	470
Cherries (tart)	270	Soybeans	3,300
Corn	13,200	Sugar Beets	6,000
		Wheat	1,320

Our Michigan Adventure

Michigan potatoes can come in many shapes!

Let's Say Thanks!

The farmers of Michigan give us much good food to eat. It is hard work to produce all this food. Most farmers often work long hours. Did you know the average farmer produces enough to feed about 125 people! We should be grateful to the farmers for the work they do for us.

Questions to think about

1. Michigan grows more of some kinds of food than any other state. Name two.

2. Where is Michigan's fruit belt? Why is it there?

3. Michigan produces much sugar. The sugar is made from what plant?

4. What is the most valuable farm business in Michigan?

Brain Stretchers

Decide which Michigan-grown food is worth the most per pound. Work in small groups to find the answer. Use information from this lesson or what you already know.

Words In Action!
Plan a menu for an all Michigan meal. Only use food which is grown in Michigan. Use a cookbook and write a recipe for one of the dishes from your menu.

These girls help pick Michigan strawberries. Courtesy Michigan State Archives.

Chapter 11   Lesson 1

Michigan's People - Who Are We?

What strengths do people from different parts
of the world give to Michigan?

Many Groups From Many Lands

It is exciting to learn about people. Michigan is home
to people from many places. Our state's people are as
different as the trees that fill our two peninsulas.

Having people from so many parts of the world is a
real advantage for Michigan. We can learn so much from
each other. We can learn about new foods and games.
We can find out about new ways of doing things. We
can share our holidays and learn about others. We are
ALL part of the Michigan family!

In the beginning this was the land of the
Native Americans. Today,
Michigan is a mixture of
many **ethnic groups**.

What About You

Before your
family came to
Michigan, where
did they live?
Everyone moved
here sometime. Do
you know in which
part of the world
your family first
lived? Was their

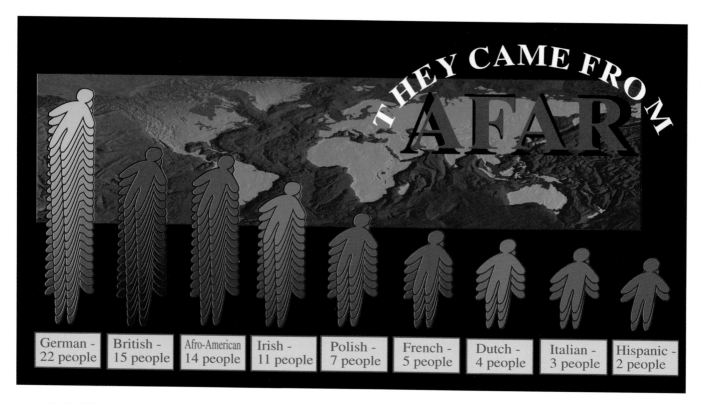

THEY CAME FROM AFAR

| German - 22 people | British - 15 people | Afro-American 14 people | Irish - 11 people | Polish - 7 people | French - 5 people | Dutch - 4 people | Italian - 3 people | Hispanic - 2 people |

Michigan's people have come from many places. If you asked 100 Michiganians where their families came from, this is what they might say. Map by Aaron Zenz.

home in a certain country? Did they move to the United States a short or long time ago?

A survey of Michigan's families will show the largest ethnic group is **German**. The second largest group has **ancestors** from Britain. Those from **Africa** are the third largest group. The **Irish** are next. Then the **Polish**, French, and **Dutch**. There are many more groups as well. Altogether, Michigan has at least 100 ethnic groups. Each has brought its own special customs with it.

The Native Americans

The Native Americans are our oldest group. Today, they live and work much as everyone else. They may work as teachers, computer programmers, builders, or artists. Some of them do live in special places. The national government set aside land just for the Michigan tribes. These places are called **reservations**.

The largest number of Native Americans live in Wayne county. So many people live in Wayne county, the same is true for many ethnic groups too. Outside of Wayne county, Chippewa county has more Native Americans than most others. Let's meet a modern Native American.

MICHIGAN'S **4** MAIN INDIAN RESERVATIONS

Shirley Brauker- Native American

Shirley Brauker was raised in the blended **traditions** of her Odawa (Ottawa) mother and her German father.

She lives in Coldwater, Michigan. Here, she has her business- Moon Bear Pottery. Shirley is an artist who makes pottery from clay. She also teaches children about her art and heritage in school programs.

A map of the Native American reservations in Michigan today. Map by Aaron Zenz.

Shirley thinks about her **heritage** as she works. Her pots have Native American designs carved into them. She often writes stories to explain each piece.

Shirley Brauker's work has been included in local and national shows and she has won many awards.

Left: Shirley Brauker. Below: One of Shirley Brauker's artistic creations. Courtesy of Shirley Brauker.

The French

The French started coming here in the late 1600s. There were not many in the beginning, but they did start Michigan's first towns.

More people with French ancestors came here during the lumbering days. They came to Michigan from Canada. They lived in the lumber towns of Saginaw, Bay City, and Muskegon.

More Settlers From Overseas

Settlers really began coming to Michigan during the 1830s. Many of the first ones were people from New York and other eastern states. In the 1840s, more settlers started to come to Michigan from Europe.

At that time food was scarce in parts of Europe. This caused people to **immigrate** or move to the United States. Many came from Germany, Ireland, Holland (or the Netherlands), and a part of England called Cornwall. Later, more people arrived from other countries.

The Germans

The chart on page 214 shows people with a German background are now the largest group in Michigan. The first families came in 1833. The Germans began to settle the Ann Arbor area and the Saginaw River valley. They also started the towns of **Frankenmuth** and **Westphalia**. The German immigrants left home because of crop failures and political problems. The famous labor leader, Walter Reuther, had German ancestors.

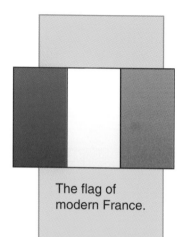

The flag of modern France.

This map shows where people with German ancestors live in Michigan. Maps by Aaron Zenz.

> **Questions to think about**
>
> 1. Name one of the four largest ethnic groups living in Michigan.
>
> 2. Do most of Michigan's Native Americans live on reservations today?
>
> 3. If a person *immigrates*, what is he or she doing?
>
> 4. Name a Michigan city which has many people with German ancestors.
>
> **Brain Stretchers**
> Which one of the four largest ethnic groups came the farthest to reach Michigan?
>
> *Words In Action!*
> Put yourself in the shoes of an immigrant of long ago. You have just arrived in Michigan. Write a letter home telling the ways life is better in Michigan. Also tell about the things you miss.

Chapter 11 Lesson 2

Are These Your Ancestors?

The British (Cornish, English, Scotch, Welsh)

The British had control of Michigan for a short time in the 1700s. There were few settlers during those years. Most of the Michigan people with British ancestors first lived in northern states near the Atlantic Ocean. They moved west to Michigan beginning in the 1830s.

A man playing the bagpipes at the Alma Scottish Festival. Courtesy Travel Michigan.

In the 1850s, Michigan mine owners needed more workers. They asked miners to come from a part of Britain called Cornwall. Most of these people moved to the U.P.

Michigan also has many people who came from Scotland long ago. The city of Alma has a Scottish festival each year.

The African Americans

Africa is a continent made up of many countries. It is a very large land. Africans do not all have the same customs or religion.

Some African Americans have lived in Michigan since the time of the French. Remember Jean de Sable who traded furs here?

Between 1830 and 1860 many escaped slaves passed through Michigan. Most of these went on to Canada, but some stayed. The southwest corner of the Lower Peninsula attracted escaped slaves. They came to begin their own farms. The towns of **Benton Harbor** and **Cassopolis** soon had many African Americans.

The largest number of African Americans came to Michigan after 1910. They left farms in the South and came here to find better jobs in our factories. African Americans helped make millions of cars and trucks. They fought in wars to protect freedom for everyone. There are African American teachers, legislators, judges, and city mayors.

AFRICA

The flag of Nigeria represents the many nations in Africa.

Dennis Archer

Hard work and sweat will bring you up the ladder of success. Ask Dennis Archer; he knows. He began his first job when he was just eight years old. Dennis worked wherever he could- a bowling alley, dish washing, sweeping the floor in a bakery.

Over the years his jobs have really changed! Recently, he was on Michigan's supreme court. He was also a teacher and a lawyer.

Dennis Archer wanted to help his city- Detroit. In 1992, he ran for the office of mayor. He won the election and did well. *Newsweek* magazine listed fomer Mayor Archer as one of the "25 Most Dynamic Mayors In America." Mr. Archer was Detroit's mayor until 2002.

Dennis Archer.
Courtesy of the Office of the Mayor.

The Irish

Many Irish came here after 1845. That was the year their potato crop failed. Potatoes were a very important food in Ireland. Disease killed the potatoes. There was much starvation in Ireland.

Detroit had a big Irish population for many years. Outside of the larger cities, the Irish settled in the Irish Hills. The Irish Hills are along U.S. 12 in southeastern Michigan.

Two famous people with Irish ancestors are Henry Ford and Frank Murphy. Henry Ford's father came from Ireland in 1847. Frank Murphy was once the governor of Michigan. He also became a member of the United States Supreme Court.

This map shows where people with Polish ancestors live in Michigan.

This map shows where people with Dutch ancestors live in Michigan.

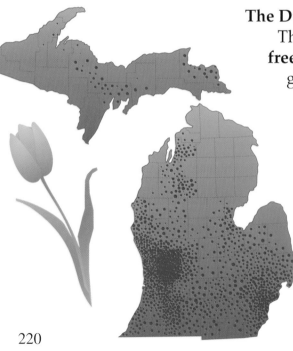

The Polish

Poland is a large country in eastern Europe. Food was often scarce in Poland. Sometimes other countries took parts of Poland for themselves. The people of Poland often saw little future in staying where they were. Some Polish people left their homeland to find better jobs.

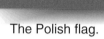

The Polish flag.

A few Polish people have been here since early times. The Godek family lived in Detroit in 1762. Most came much later. When they reached Michigan they wanted to have farms. It was often the work they knew best. They helped start small towns like **Bronson** and **Posen**. Bronson has a Polish festival each summer.

Later, many Polish people went to work in the car factories. They moved into towns like **Hamtramck** and worked in the Dodge plant.

The Dutch

The Dutch came to find **religious freedom**. In the 1840s, the Dutch government took control of the church. This may sound like a strange idea to us. Many people in Holland did not like the government running the church. Since they could not change the government, these people left the country.

Reverend Albertus Van Raalte led the first Dutch settlers to America. They arrived in western Michigan in 1847 and started **Holland**, Michigan.

220

Michigan Cities with Well-Known ETHNIC groups

Hancock
Ishpeming
Iron River
Iron Mountain
Norway
Posen

- ● **African**
- ○ **Arabic**
- ○ **Dutch**
- ○ **Finnish**
- ● **German**
- ● **Greek**
- ○ **Irish**
- ● **Norwegian**
- ● **Polish**
- ○ **Scotch**
- ● **Swedish**

Alma
Grand Rapids
Frankenmuth
Zeeland
Westphalia
Holland
Hamtrack
Dearborn
Greektown
Benton Harbor
Irish Hills
Cassopolis
Bronson

Grand Rapids also has many people with a Dutch background as does **Zeeland**.

Several people of Dutch background have held important political jobs. Arthur Vandenberg was a United States Senator from Michigan. He helped start the United Nations.

Walter Chrysler was another person with Dutch ancestors. He started one of the great car companies in the 1920s.

The Hispanic

This group covers a large number of people from many countries. Most of the Hispanic people in Michigan have come from three places. One is **Mexico**, the country just south of the United States. Another is **Puerto Rico**. The third is **Cuba**. Cuba and Puerto Rico are large islands.

In the early years, there were few Hispanic people in Michigan. For example, the first Hispanic family came to Flint in 1914. But, by the 1920s, several thousand Hispanic people were helping harvest crops in Michigan.

Often Hispanic people first came to Michigan to help pick crops. Courtesy of Michigan State Archives

As these people learned more about Michigan, they found better jobs. Let us learn more about two successful Hispanic people.

Miguel Navarro came to Michigan and worked hard to succeed. He and his wife have built a growing business making tortillas and tortilla chips. Courtesy Miguel Navarro.

Dr. Gumecindo Salas teaches at Michigan State University. He has also been on the state board of education. Courtesy of Dr. Gumecindo Salas.

Miguel "Mike" Navarro

For many Hispanic people, life in Michigan meant hard work. In 1948, Miguel Navarro labored in the celery fields for 60 cents an hour. His wife, Isabel, worked beside him.

It took several years to find a good job. Then in 1977, Mr. Navarro purchased an empty building and a tortilla machine. He began making tortillas and taco chips for Mexican restaurants. The business became very successful.

Miguel and Isabel are quick to encourage other Hispanics. He says "Life, it's been a struggle, but there is no day that passes by that I don't thank the Lord. Thank him for the little bit that I have."

Gumecindo Salas

Gumecindo Salas grew up in the thumb area of Michigan. He began school in a one-room school house, but he went a long way from there. Finally, he earned a Ph.D. from the University of Michigan.

In 1976, Dr. Salas was elected to the State Board of Education. From 1982 to 1984, he was the board's president. The board of education is in charge of all the schools in Michigan. Now Dr. Salas is an assistant professor at Michigan State University.

Dr. Salas cares about Michigan's students. He works to be sure that everyone has a chance to graduate from high school. He tells students how important it is to get a good education.

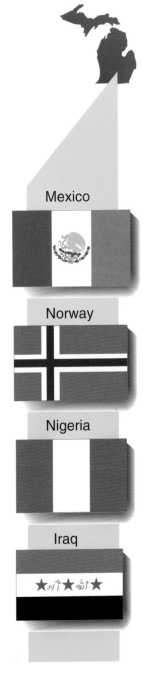

Questions to think about

1. Give three reasons why people have moved to Michigan from other countries.

2. Tell about some of the jobs immigrants did when they first reached Michigan.

3. Match the cities with their important ethnic group:

Hamtramck	Dutch
Cassopolis	Scotch
Zeeland	African American
Alma	Polish

4. During which years did escaped slaves sometimes move to Michigan?

5. Name a well-known African American who lived in Michigan.

6. What kinds of scarcity caused people to leave their homelands? (What was scarce at home?)

Brain Stretchers
Why didn't many people from other countries move to Michigan before the 1830s?

Words In Action!
Make your own crossword puzzle using the names of Michigan's ethnic groups.

Write about someone in this chapter whom you like. Tell what you like about this person and some things about his or her life.

Having many people from many lands gives Michigan diversity. (Diversity sounds like- dih VER seh tee.) Diversity is a core democratic value. It means having many kinds of culture, ethnic background, race, lifestyle and belief. This is not only allowed, but is desired. Diversity is good for our society. It makes us stronger, not weaker.

Chapter 11 Lesson 3

More Nations in Our Parade of Ancestors

The Italians

The French and the **Italians** were the first people to come here from Europe. Alphonse de Tonty came to Detroit in 1701 with Cadillac. De Tonty's daughter was the first European born in Detroit! Later, many more Italians came to work in the Upper Peninsula's mines.

The Swedish

Swedish people started to come to Michigan after the Civil War. They discovered the Upper Peninsula was like their own country in many ways. They began to work in the mines and lumber camps.

Ishpeming, **Iron River**, and **Iron Mountain** are cities with many Swedish people.

Michigan's longest serving governor also had Swedish ancestors. William Milliken served as governor for fourteen years.

The Swedish flag.

The Finnish

The people from Finland first came to work in our copper and iron mines. That was in 1864. They also worked in the logging camps. **Hancock**, Michigan has a college started by the Finnish.

Later on, Finnish people came to Detroit. The Saarinen family helped develop the Cranbrook

This map shows where people with Finnish heritage live in Michigan

Academy. Cranbrook is a well-known school near Detroit. Eliel Saarinen (el EE el SAHR uh nen) was a famous architect. An architect designs buildings.

Eliel Saarinen was a famous Finnish architect. He designed many buildings. This picture shows one of those buildings. Art by Aaron Zenz.

The Arabic

Among all the states, Michigan has one of the largest groups of Arabic people. They live in cities near Detroit-cities like Dearborn and **Southfield.**

Arabic people come from many countries, not just Saudi Arabia. Actually most have come to Michigan from **Iraq**, **Jordan**, **Lebanon**, and **Syria**.

Many people living in the Arab world believe in the **Muslim religion**. However, quite a number of those living in Michigan are Christians.

Former United States Senator Spencer Abraham is one of those. He represented Michigan in Washington, D.C. where he was the only Arab-American in the U.S. Senate.

Casey Kasem is a famous Arab-American radio disk jockey and television personality. Kasem was born in Detroit. Each year Detroit holds an Arab World Festival.

The flag of Iraq.

Albert Kahn was a famous architech.

Jewish Americans

Fur trading brought many people to Michigan. One was Ezekiel Solomon. He came to Mackinac Island in 1761. Ezekiel was the first known Jewish settler in Michigan. Chapman Abraham was Detroit's first Jewish settler. These men lived in exciting times. Both were captured by the Indians near Detroit during Pontiac's Rebellion of 1763.

Other Jewish families settled in Adrian, Monroe, and **Three Rivers**. More Jewish settlers arrived in Michigan between 1880 and 1914.

Albert Kahn was a well-known architect. He designed many factories and other buildings in the 1920s and 1930s.

Many people of Jewish heritage have been politicians and judges. Charles Levin was a member of the state supreme court. Carl Levin was a U.S. Senator from Michigan for many years.

The Japanese

Most people with Japanese heritage moved to Michigan after World War II. One of these was a young architect named Minoru Yamasaki (min or oo yam ah sock ee). He worked in Detroit and began to design attractive buildings. Yamaski's greatest achievement was the design of the World Trade Center in New York City.

In the last few years, a number of families from Japan came to Michigan to manage some of the new Japanese car parts companies. You might meet these Japanese in places like Battle Creek, Detroit, and Kalamazoo.

These are only a few of the ethnic groups from Michigan. There are many more you can study.

More People Facts

Michigan is the eighth largest state in population. We have about 10,000,000 people. Michigan's people are concentrated in certain parts of the state. Most live in the southern third of the Lower Peninsula.

In fact, four out of ten Michigan people live in three counties! They are Wayne, Oakland, and Macomb.

It is interesting to know the three counties added together have more people than over 25 of our other states. With so many people, these counties influence much of what happens in Michigan.

Two girls dressed in the costume of their ancestors. Courtesy of Michigan State Archives

Map on next page: Most of Michigan's people live in the southeastern corner of the state. Map by Aaron Zenz.

Questions to think about

1. Some people from this country came with the French in the early 1700s. Name it.

2. William Milliken had ancestors from which country?

3. Choose someone mentioned in this chapter. Write a short biography about him or her. Tell about his or her ethnic background.

4. Rewrite this paragraph with the correct facts.

   Michigan is the state with the largest population. We have over 12,000,000 people. Most of them live in the northeast Lower Peninsula near Alpena.

Brain Stretchers

You have read about some of the groups of people who have moved to Michigan in the past. Who do you think will move to Michigan in the future? Why do you think they will come?

Words In Action!

You are writing a magazine article on the good points of living in Michigan. Focus on how Michigan's many ethnic groups help make Michigan a more interesting place to live.

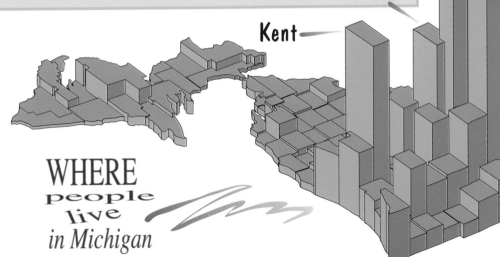

Wayne

Oakland

Macomb

Genesee

Kent

WHERE
people
live
in Michigan

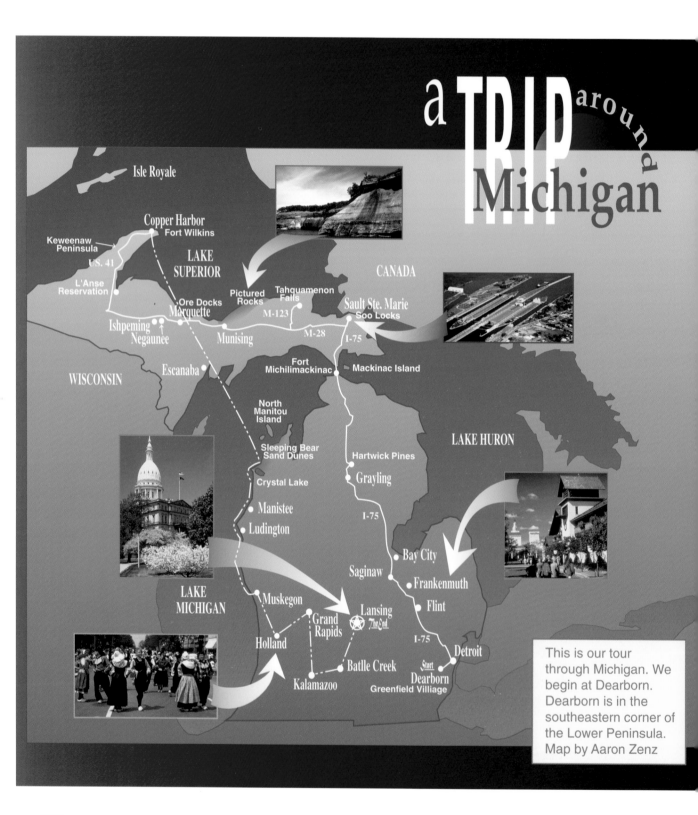

a **TRIP** around Michigan

Isle Royale

Copper Harbor
Fort Wilkins

Keweenaw
Peninsula
US. 41

LAKE
SUPERIOR

L'Anse
Reservation

Ore Docks
Marquette

Ishpeming
Negaunee

Munising

Pictured
Rocks

Tahquamenon
Falls

M-123

M-28

I-75

CANADA

Sault Ste. Marie
Soo Locks

Escanaba

WISCONSIN

Fort
Michilimackinac

Mackinac Island

North
Manitou
Island

LAKE HURON

Sleeping Bear
Sand Dunes

Crystal Lake

Hartwick Pines

Grayling

Manistee

Ludington

I-75

LAKE
MICHIGAN

Muskegon

Holland

Grand
Rapids

Lansing
The End

Saginaw

Bay City

Frankenmuth

Flint

I-75

Detroit

Kalamazoo

Battle Creek

Start
Dearborn
Greenfield Villiage

This is our tour
through Michigan. We
begin at Dearborn.
Dearborn is in the
southeastern corner of
the Lower Peninsula.
Map by Aaron Zenz

228

Chapter 12 Lesson 1

So Much To See In Michigan!

What attracts people to vacation and travel in Michigan?

Sharing About Places to Visit

Suppose your family has a visitor from another country or a faraway state. You would probably like to show your guest some of the interesting places in Michigan. Your family says let's go. It is up to you to plan the trip. Where will you go? How are you going to get there?

Art by Theresa Deeter.

Our Highways

Before you start planning, you need to know about Michigan's roads and **interstate highways**.

These highways are called interstates because they go from one state to another. Three main interstate highways in Michigan are I-75, I-96 and I-94. They all have the "I" for interstate. Those with odd numbers, like 75, go mostly north and south. Those with even numbers go mostly east and west.

Michigan's Main Cities and Highways

stands for an interstate like I-75

stands for a Michigan route like M-22

Larger dots stand for larger cities with more people.

75 goes south to Florida

229

Highways built by the state have an "M" in the name, such as M-23. There are also roads with U.S. in the name. These go across the United States. US-2 and US-12 are examples.

When you look on a map, the highway numbers are in circles or **shields** like this:

state roads ⭕   U.S. roads. ⬭   interstate highways. 🛡️

Your Michigan Tour

Now let's visit several of the popular places chosen by tourists. Find your map and get ready!

The Henry Ford museum. The museum has thousands of items for visitors to see. Courtesy Henry Ford Museum and Greenfield Village.

Start At Dearborn

We will start in Dearborn, which is near Detroit. Dearborn is the home of the Ford Motor Company. Henry Ford's old home is here. **Greenfield Village** and the **Henry Ford Museum** are in Dearborn too.

The Henry Ford museum has airplanes and steam engines inside. It has many early cars and machines.

Greenfield Village has houses and famous buildings from many places. These buildings were taken apart and moved to Dearborn. Thomas Edison's lab is here. You can see where the Wright brothers worked on their airplane. There is a train which goes through the village. Look, here comes the riverboat around the bend!

The shop where the Wright brothers made the first airplane has been moved to Greenfield Village in Dearborn, MI.

Another museum has opened in Dearborn. It is the **Automotive Hall of Fame**. You can find it on Oakwood Boulevard. This museum is one more clue telling you this part of Michigan had much to do with developing the car.

Downtown In Motown

Now we will travel east on US-12 to reach downtown Detroit. Detroit has tall, tall buildings. The Renaissance Center is one of the tallest. It has a hotel and the headquarters for General Motors.

Detroit also has the **Motown Museum**. This is a great stop if you like the music once made there in "Studio A." Motown had some outstanding performers like the Supremes, Stevie Wonder, and Smokey Robinson.

One of Detroit's newest museums is the **Museum of African American History**. It has some very interesting displays. Discover the accomplishments of African Americans in Michigan and the nation. There is much to see including a life-sized section of a slave ship.

Detroit's Renaissance Center. Courtesy Don Sinonelli and Travel Michigan.

Near Flint- the Vehicle City

For the next part of our trip, we will go north on I-75. Just past Flint is **Crossroads Village.** Here you can step right back in time. The village has 29 buildings set up to be just as they were between 1860 and 1880.

Frankenmuth, Michigan. A little of Germany moved to Michigan. Courtesy Bronner's Christmas. Wonderland.

German Heritage

It is time to leave and get on I-75. Let's go to Frankenmuth for lunch! It is well known for good places to eat. Frankenmuth is a town where many of the people have German ancestors. It is a top tourist stop. Every June Frankenmuth has a German festival.

Our Michigan Adventure

At the Straits

By going north on I-75 you reach the Mackinac Bridge. We should arrive about the time they turn on the lights. At night the bridge is quite a sight! It is hundreds of feet above the water. Ships sail by far beneath it.

Mackinac Bridge. Courtesy Michigan Travel.

Next to the south end of the bridge is a fort. This is Fort Michilimackinac. It is the fort that was captured by Chief Pontiac's warriors in the 1750s. Fort Michilimackinac often has actors dressed as in the old times.

As we drive north across the bridge, look to the right. You can see Mackinac Island. It is the small island nearby. Fort Mackinac is on the island. It is a large white fort on top of a hill. Can you see it?

Mackinac Island is an unusual place to visit. There are no cars on the island. They are not allowed. Everyone uses horses, wagons, or bicycles!

The Soo Locks

I-75 goes across the Upper Peninsula. It is about fifty miles to Sault St. Marie, which is also called "the Soo."

The Soo is next to Canada. On one side is Lake Superior. On the other side is Lake Huron. The Soo Locks are in between. These are the locks that thousands of ships use. Remember, the locks are needed because Lake Superior is

The Soo Locks from the air. Courtesy Travel Michigan. A ship being lowered by a lock. Dave McConnell

higher than Lake Huron. You can stand at the edge of the locks and watch the ships go by.

The Roaring Water

We begin to travel west on M-28. After about thirty miles, we will turn north on M-123. By going on this road, we can reach Tahquamenon Falls. It is the second largest waterfall east of the Mississippi River! The falls are on the Tahquamenon River as it flows east. The river empties into Lake Superior.

Tahquamenon Falls. Courtesy Thomas A. Schneider and Travel Michigan.

Questions to think about

1. Tell about two things a person can see in or near Detroit.

2. Which of these interstate highways go north and south, and which go east and west: I-75, I-96 and I-94?

3. Give directions to reach Tahquamenon Falls from your hometown. Use highway numbers and compass directions.

Brain Stretchers
Use a mileage key and tell how far it is to the Mackinac Bridge from each of these places:

Dearborn, Flint, Grayling

Words In Action!
Choose the place in this lesson which is the most interesting to you. Write a tourist brochure that tells about your choice.

This is how downtown Detroit looked about 1905.
Courtesy Library of Congress.

Chapter 12 Lesson 2

Finishing Our Tour Of Michigan

Pictured Rocks along the north shore of the Upper Peninsula. Courtesy Travel Michigan.

Starting on M-28 again, we come to Munising. Munising is on the edge of Lake Superior. People have visited the rocks along the shore since the time of the French explorers. High rock cliffs line the shore and the rocks are streaked with many colors. The area is called the **Pictured Rocks.**

Before long, we will come to Marquette. It is 165 miles from the Soo. Marquette is along the shore of Lake Superior. There are iron mines near Marquette.

Copper Country

Highway M-28 heads west. After a while it meets US-41. Highway US-41 goes north. The highway goes through **L'Anse** Reservation. Soon, we will be on the Keweenaw Peninsula. At the tip is **Copper Harbor**. Early copper miners worked here. There is also a fort. This is **Fort Wilkins**. It was built in 1844 during the early copper mining days.

The Big Island

About 50 miles northwest across the deep blue water is Isle Royale. Isle Royale is a national park. It is a land of trees, moose, and wolves! In the summer, boats take

Fort Wilkins is near the northern tip of Michigan. Courtesy Travel Michigan.

Chapter 12 *So Much to See in Michigan!*

Art by Charles Schafer. Courtesy of the Michigan Department of Natural Resources.

people to hike and camp on the island. They often look for moose. Campers can also hear wolves call at night!

What a Sand Dune!

Let's use a small airplane for the rest of our trip. Up we go! The pilot will take us across the U.P. We are headed toward the Lower Peninsula and the **Sleeping Bear Sand Dunes**.

Below us are the green forests of the Upper Peninsula. After a while, we will reach Escanaba. The plane will soon be over the water of Lake Michigan.

The giant Sleeping Bear sand dune. Courtesy Nancy Hanatyk.

As we near the far shore, we can see two islands. These are North and South **Manitou Islands**. They are part of the Sleeping Bear Dunes National Lakeshore.

Soon we can see the huge dunes. This is a very big hill of sand. There is only sand almost as far as the eye can see! It has this name because the tribes have a legend about how the dune was formed. Do you know the story?

The Holland Tulip Festival. Michael M. Smith and Travel Michigan.

Holland- Michigan

Before long, we can look down and see a big windmill. Now we know we are at Holland, Michigan. The windmill is called DeZwaan and its name means "the swan." It was moved across the Atlantic Ocean from the country of Holland in Europe. Many Dutch people moved to this city years ago. Holland, Michigan has a large tulip festival each spring.

235

The Second Largest City

It is time for the plane to turn east. We will fly to Grand Rapids. Grand Rapids has two big museums

downtown. One is in honor of past President Gerald Ford. This is his hometown. Inside the museum you can see many things about President Ford including a copy of the Oval Office from the White House. It is just like it was when he used it in Washington, D.C. Mr. Ford was President from 1974 to 1977.

This is the Gerald Ford Presidential Museum in Grand Rapids. Courtesy David McConnell.

The other museum is the **Van Andel Museum Center**. Here you can see what it was like to live in Grand Rapids years ago. You can walk down an old street and visit the stores. You can learn all about how furniture was made and the different jobs workers did. This museum even has a real **carrousel**! It also has a very good display about Michigan's Native Americans.

Kalamazoo

Our pilot says we must make a stop at the Kalamazoo Air Zoo. If she says it is good, we must stop! Actually it is the **Kalamazoo Aviation History Museum**. This museum has several planes including a Ford tri-motor plane. Once the Ford company even made airplanes! This plane has three engines! Some days they take it out and fly it.

The Cereal City

Let's go to Battle Creek. You can't visit the cereal factories anymore, but you can visit the new cereal museum! Here you can learn all about the history of breakfast cereal in Battle Creek.

While you visit Battle Creek, don't miss the **Binder Park Zoo**. There are many animals here. You can even feed some of them. Don't look over your shoulder. That is a full-sized dinosaur model standing there!

Wave to the Governor!

Our plane will land in Lansing, the state capital. The big white dome of the capitol building can be seen for miles. This is where the governor works. Our state laws are made in the capitol.

You can visit the capitol building. You can walk by the door of the governor's office. Perhaps you can peek inside! If the members of the state house or senate are meeting, you can watch them from the second floor.

Michigan' state capitol.
Courtesy Travel Michigan.

Lansing Has REAL HISTORY

Lansing also has some good museums. Each one is different; you will never see the same thing twice! There is the **Michigan Women's Historical Center and Hall of Fame.** It is about a mile south of the capitol.

Another museum is the **Michigan Historical Museum**. Its building also has the state library and the state archives. Many of the pictures for this book came from the state archives!

The Michigan Historical Museum is a neat place. Inside you can see part of a copper mine. The explosives are in the rock and the fuses ready to light! You can touch real "big wheels" like the lumberjacks used. You can learn about the labor unions and the strikes. You can see part of a B-24 bomber- the ones made in Michigan during World War II. This is REAL HISTORY!

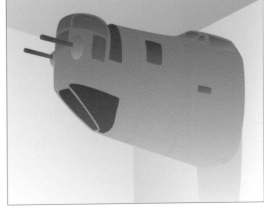

The Michigan Historical Museum even has part of a B-24 bomber from World War II.

Tourists Are Big Business

It costs money to have a vacation. Tourists and travelers spend about $15 billion a year in Michigan. They spend money at motels, restaurants, gas stations and gift shops. This brings income to the people who run these businesses. Travel and tourism give jobs to about 300,000 Michiganians.

Be Proud!

Be proud that Michigan is your home. Tell others about the state where you live. Tell your class about places where YOU have visited.

See Michigan!

Questions to think about

1. Plan a trip including three interesting Michigan places. Organize your trip. Tell which place you would visit first, second, and third.

2. Write each of the following places on your paper. Next to it write L.P. or U.P. for the peninsula where it is located.

- Sleeping Bear Sand Dune
- Greenfield Village
- Soo Locks
- Pictured Rocks
- Motown Museum
- Kalamazoo Aviation History Museum

3. Give three reasons why people visit Michigan.

Brain Stretchers

Make a word game using places in this chapter. The words must link in this way- the last letter of the first word must be used as the first letter of the second word and so forth.

Words In Action!

Create a travel brochure inviting people to visit places in Michigan for each season- summer, fall, winter, and spring.

Chapter 13   Lesson 1

It Happens In Lansing- Our State Government

Which of our needs does government take care of
and how does it take care of them?

Why Do We Have Government?

Let us go back in time a little over 100 years ago. A man and his wife were going down a country road in their horse and buggy. They reached a small bridge and began to go across. Suddenly the bridge gave way! The man, the lady, the horse, and the buggy all splashed into the river. No one was hurt, but this certainly ruined their trip.

The people were surprised, but not that surprised. The bridge looked quite rundown. Why was the bridge in such bad condition? Who was supposed to take care of the bridge? This is the point of the true story. No one was in charge of taking care of the bridge!

Many years earlier a farmer had built the bridge. He spent his own money to do the job and took care of it for a while. For years no one else offered to help. Finally he got tired of doing the repairs and stopped.

At that time, no part of Michigan government was in charge of building and repairing roads! Can you imagine how hard it would be to travel today if that were still true?

This story points out why we have government. It tells about one kind of service government can do for the people. It would be very hard to have good roads if each person took care of the road in front of his or her home. That is the way it used to be!

Government provides services which are hard for people to do themselves. Government builds roads, schools, some hospitals, runs courts, and provides police. It also makes our **laws**.

Laws are rules to live by. We have laws so people will be safe and can have a good life. Laws help keep people from doing things they should not do.

Most laws are common sense. People should be nice and not do things which hurt or bother others. Sadly, many people think only of themselves. People drive too fast, throw junk along the roads, cheat others, and pollute the air.

 **National Washington, D.C.**   **State Lansing, MI**

The Two Main Divisions of Government

The two main groups are state government and national government. Sometimes the national government is called the **federal government**.

We have a national government to make laws for the United States. The national government also runs the army, navy, air force, and so forth. It makes treaties with other countries. It prints our money and makes our coins. The national government is at Washington, D.C. The leader of the national government is the President of the United States.

We have a state government to take care of things at the state level. The state government makes the state laws.

It takes care of state highways. It tells people how old they must be to drive. It is in charge of the state police. It provides rules for all the schools in the state. The state capital is in Lansing. The governor is the leader of our state government.

Being Close To The Situation

If government is to work well, it must be close to the people. We have city governments to work closely with people on city problems. It would not be easy to have every city problem taken care of by someone in Lansing. They might not really understand the problem because they did not live close to it.

Paying For Government

Who pays for the cost of government? Each kind of government gets money from **taxes.** Taxes pay wages for the police, fire fighters, road builders, and teachers.

Michigan has a **sales tax** which you pay when you buy most things. It is six percent or six cents on each dollar. If you pay $100 for roller blades, the tax is $6.00.

Everyone who works in Michigan also pays an **income tax**. This is a tax on the money they earn. Businesses also pay taxes to state government. Some cities also have sales and income taxes.

Another important tax is the **property tax**. Home owners and businesses pay taxes every year on the value of their land and buildings.

Whenever we buy anything in Michigan we must pay a sales tax. The only exceptions are groceries and medicine. Art by Aaron Zenz.

Questions to think about

1. Which is true about a law?
    a. A law is a rule to be ignored.
     b. A law is a rule to live by.
       c. A law is a rule which should be broken.

2. Give one good reason why we need to have laws.

3. How does government get the money it needs?

4. What is a sales tax? How much is Michigan's sales tax?

Brain Stretchers
Explain what limits the amount of money government can spend.

Words In Action!
Explain what services governments can provide.

Voting is very important. If people do not vote, they let someone else decide for them. The right to vote is part of a core democratic value called *popular sovereignty. (sounds like- SOV er en tee)* See page 251.

Chapter 13 Lesson 2

More About How It Works

How Is Government Controlled?

What do you do if you think there are too many taxes or too much waste? **Voting** is the way people control what government does. To be able to vote in Michigan, you must be 18 years old and live in the state. The process of voting is called an **election**.

We have elections for the President, the governor, mayors, judges, and many others in government. The elections for each office are at a certain time. We vote for the President of the United States every four years. Michigan's governor is also elected every four years. The election for governor is held on different years than the one for President. We will vote for our governor in 2002, 2006, 2010 and so forth.

Besides elections, there is another way government is controlled. This is with the **constitution**. The constitution is a written set of rules. It says what government can do and how it can do it. It is like the rule book for government.

We have a constitution for the national government and one for the state government too. Cities and counties also have documents like constitutions, but they have different names.

The Michigan constitution was written when we first became a state. That was a very long time ago. Because things change over so many years, it is possible to make changes to the constitution. Several changes have been made to the Michigan constitution. These changes are called **amendments**. But it is not easy to make those changes. Since the constitution is very important, it is hard to change it on a whim.

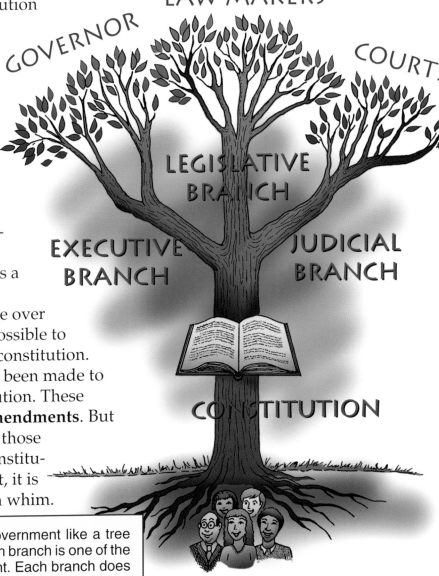

Some people think of government like a tree with three branches. Each branch is one of the three parts of government. Each branch does a different job.

243

Who Decides What It Means?

What happens if people in government do not agree on what the constitution means? This does happen. Then it is the job of the **supreme court** to decide. Michigan has its own supreme court and so does the national government. The supreme court is a very important part of our system of government.

The supreme court in Michigan has seven judges called justices. Voters in Michigan elect the judges on the supreme court.

Michigan State Supreme Court. Courtesy Office of Court Administrator.

The Supreme Court Is Special

The supreme court is not like other courts. They deal with only the most important cases. The seven justices decide which cases they will hear. All the justices listen to each case at the same time. There are no juries in the supreme court. In the supreme court, the justices all vote to decide each case.

The U. S. supreme court decides what the United States constitution means. It also decides what national laws mean.

Other Courts Are Needed

Besides the state supreme court, Michigan has other kinds of courts too. Each county has a courthouse. One or more courts are held there. The person in charge of each court is a judge. Since this branch has many judges, it is also called the **judicial branch**.

Unlike the Michigan Supreme Court, most other courts have a jury which helps decide right or wrong. Being on a jury is another way we take part in government. Jury members are selected from people living in Michigan. Perhaps one of your parents has served on a jury.

State Government Has Three Parts

1

2

3

State government has three parts. The courts are one part. They decide the law. A second part enforces the laws and the third part makes the laws. Having these three parts separates the power of government. This way no one part has too much power. We call this "separation of powers."

If government is like a tree with three branches, then the trunk might be the constitution. It is the constitution which holds up the tree and makes it strong. We call following the written rules of the constitution going by the "rule of law."

The roots of the tree might be the voters. Without the voters, or roots, the tree would dry up and die.

The Governor's Branch Enforces the Laws

We have talked about one branch- the courts. Another branch enforces the laws. Of course this branch has the state police. Actually, there is much more to this branch than the police. The governor is in this branch too. He or she is in

A group of Michigan State Police officers. Courtesy Michigan State Police.

this branch because the governor controls many departments that deal with laws and rules. Some of these departments are environmental quality, consumer and industry services, and of course the state police. The governor's branch is also called the **executive branch** and it has nearly 20 departments.

Who Makes Our State Laws?

The state laws for Michigan are made in Lansing. The place where they are made is the **capitol building.** The people who do this are called lawmakers or **legislators**.

The lawmakers are divided into two groups. One group works in the **state senate**. The other group works in the **state house of representatives**. Representative means to represent or act in place of another person. Because most people are busy working in their jobs, they cannot go to Lansing to make laws.

We vote for representatives and senators to do that for us. Having someone else represent us, means we have "representative government."

The state senate and house of representatives both meet in the capitol building, but not together. Each group has its own large room where they meet.

Whom Does Each Lawmaker Represent?

Michigan is divided into many parts called districts. There are districts for those in the senate and for those in the house. There are 110 house districts and 38 senate districts. Each district elects its own person. This means Michigan has 148 lawmakers! We have many districts so the people elected from each one will be close to its problems.

Art by Theresa Deeter.

Questions to think about

1. Match the item on the left with the best choice on the right. Write them on your paper.

1. Election-	a. the rule book for government
2. Constitution-	b. judges decide what the constitution means
3. Supreme court-	c. choosing people with a vote
4. The governor-	d. executive branch
5. Lawmakers-	e. judicial branch
6. Courts-	f. are members of the house or senate

2. Is it possible to ever change Michigan's constitution? Tell what you have learned about changing the state constitution.

3. How does separation of powers work in our state government?

Words In Action!
Work in small groups. Write an idea for a new law or a change in one we already have.

Chapter 13 Lesson 3

Making Laws and More!

Each new law begins as an idea. People tell their ideas to the state senator or representative for their district. One of the lawmakers will write a **bill.** A bill is the official wording of the idea for a new law. The lawmakers will talk about the bill in the house or in the senate. Then they will vote on the bill. If the bill passes, it will go to the other group of lawmakers. Finally, if both groups pass the bill, it goes to the governor.

The Governor Has the Final Vote

The governor can sign the bill. If it is signed, it will become law. But suppose the governor does not like the bill. The governor can **veto** the bill. This usually means the bill will never become law. The use of the veto is a powerful tool for the governor.

Art by Theresa Deeter.

Review the three branches of state government.

1. Governor's branch or the executive branch
   leads the state and enforces laws
2. Lawmaker's branch or the legislative branch
   has two groups called the house and the senate which make our state laws
3. Courts or the judicial branch
   the supreme court decides what the laws mean. Other courts hear different kinds of cases.

Government can be complicated. There are different layers inside one another. It can be like this kangaroo with smaller kangaroos inside its pouch. Art by Aaron Zenz.

The boxes below show the same idea.

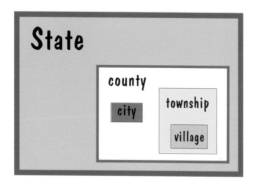

City and County Government

Each city and each county also has its own government. The **mayor** leads city government working with a **city council**. Counties are usually run by groups called **county commissions**.

MICHIGAN HAS **83** COUNTY GOVERNMENTS

City government and county government work with local matters. The state government deals with problems which usually affect the whole state. The national or **federal** government deals with matters affecting the whole country or several states.

Our system of government is complex. We have not told you about all the steps and things which take place. Almost everything we have talked about for Michigan government is the same in other states too. The national government in Washington, D. C., works in much the same way. The biggest difference is that we have the President instead of the governor.

The Voters

The voters do not usually get big headlines in the news. Still, they are the most important part of the government. In the United States everyone who is old enough can vote. Voting is a great opportunity. When people do not vote, they are letting others make choices for them.

There are things you can do even if you are not old enough to vote. You can write letters and send e-mail to the governor or lawmakers and give your opinion. You can tell what you think should be done. Here is an example of young people in action.

Letter writer and deer by Theresa Deeter.

Students from Borculo Christian School near Grand Rapids wanted Michigan to have a state mammal. They contacted the state representative from their area. They told about their idea. They wanted the whitetail deer to be the state mammal.

The students went to Lansing to hear the lawmakers in the house of representatives talk about it. Some lawmakers were for the idea and some were not. Many people like the whitetail deer, but the deer also eat crops and can be pests.

Their efforts, however, were successful. On June 11, 1997, Governor Engler signed the bill making the whitetail deer our state game mammal.

Photo courtesy of the office of State Representative Jessie F. Dalman.

Questions to think about

1. What do we officially call the idea for a new law?

2. What does the word "veto" mean?

3. Compare the kinds of issues state government deals with to those dealt with by the federal government.

4. Match the terms below with the level or kind of government. Move the words on the right so they match.

1. mayor	a. national or federal
2. President	b. state
3. county commission	c. city
4. governor	d. county

Brain Stretchers

Give your opinion. Which core democratic value is most important to you. Clearly explain your answer.

Explain how popular sovereignty works in our system of government.

Words In Action!

Write your opinion for or against having the whitetail deer as the state game mammal. Everyone read your opinion to the class. Then rewrite your opinion and improve it.

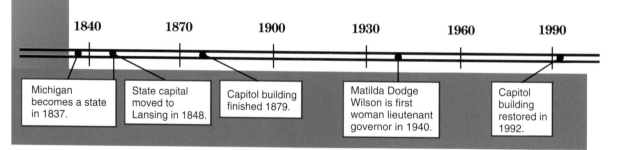

1840	1870	1900	1930	1960	1990

Michigan becomes a state in 1837.

State capital moved to Lansing in 1848.

Capitol building finished 1879.

Matilda Dodge Wilson is first woman lieutenant governor in 1940.

Capitol building restored in 1992.

State Government Time Line

～ *Important Values in Our Government* ～

The core of our government is based on some key values. We call them *core democratic values*. These are the ideas behind our state and national (federal) constitutions.

-*Life*: Our right to live. This cannot be taken away by any government unless convicted of a very serious crime.

-*Liberty*: Freedom to do as we wish as long as it does not harm anyone else. Example: We are free to travel to Lansing any time we wish.

-*Pursuit of Happiness*: Allowed to do what makes us happy, as long as it does not harm anyone else. (Pursuit sounds like: per SOOT)

-*Common Good*: Working together to make life better for everyone. Example: Girl Scouts picking up trash along the road.

-*Justice*: Everyone has the same legal rights. These include not being arrested unless charged with a crime. The right to a trial by a jury for serious crimes.

-*Equality*: People of any age, sex or color being treated the same. (Equality sounds like: ee KWAL uh tee) Example: Your teacher calling on the same number of boys and girls.

-*Diversity*: People having many differences yet working together. (Diversity sounds like: dih VER seh tee) Example: Antonio is Italian American and Giji is Native American, but they still enjoy working on school projects together.

-*Truth*: Being honest and trustworthy. Examples: Reporting the news correctly, not cheating someone in a game or in a business deal.

-*Popular Sovereignty*: The right to vote. The people have the final say in government. (Sovereignty sounds like: SOV er en tee) Example: Voters can recall a lawmaker and vote him or her from office.

-*Patriotism*: Love for our country and its values. Example: Taking time to vote or working to see there is justice for everyone. (Patriotism sounds like: PAY tree uh tiz em)

-*Religious Freedom*: The right to go to church or not to go to church. Example: The government cannot say it is against the law to go to church.

-*Right to Peacefully Assemble*: People can get together and talk about things which bother them or to tell the government what they want.

～ *Constitutional principles of the United States* ～

Our nation is ruled by written laws which have been made over many years, not by whims of those in power (The rule of law). Each of the three branches has its own duties which another branch cannot take over (Separation of powers). The people vote to elect others to represent them in government (Representative government). The President, not army officers, has final control of the military (Civilian control of the military).

The Glossary

> The glossary is a place to look if you do not understand how to say a word or what it means. These words are in bold print in the book. Some other words have been added which you might need when reading about Michigan.

acre (Aker)- a measure of land which is a square about 209 feet on each side.

Adrian (A dree un)- [Lenawee County] Population 22,000. Home of the famous Croswell Opera House. Southeast LP.

advertise (ad ver tize)- the way a business calls attention to its products.

Africa (AF rih KA)- the world's second largest continent. People from here were brought to America as slaves.

Alaska (ah las ka)- the 49th state of the United States. Alaska is located in the extreme upper northwest section of North America. It is about 60 miles from Asia with Russia being the nearest Asian country.

Alpena (al-PEE-na) [Alpena County] Population 11,400. Home of a very large cement making plant. On Thunder Bay. Northeast LP.

ambassador (am bass ah door)- a person sent by a government to be its chief representative in another country.

amendment- a change in a law or constitution. It is difficult to change the state constitution but it has been done several times over the years. Since 1963 about 20 changes have been made and about 30 turned down.

American Revolution (rev oh LOO shun)- the war between the British and the American colonies (1775-1783). The colonies gained their freedom to rule themselves. They started the United States.

ammunition (AM you ni shun)- bullets and cannon shells, etc.

ancestors (ann CES terz)- relatives from long ago like great grandparents, and so on.

Anishnabek (ah NISH na bek)- an Ojibwa word meaning first people.

Ann Arbor [Washtenaw County] Population 109,600. Home of University of Michigan. Much scientific research is done in Ann Arbor. Southeast LP.

archaeologist (ar key AL uh jist)- a person who studies how people lived long ago by digging up and examining tools, weapons, dishes, bones, pottery, fossils, and other clues.

Arsenal of Democracy (ARS en al)- name given to Michigan because it was among the top states in making equipment such as airplanes and tanks for World War II. An arsenal is a place to make or store weapons.

Asia- a very large continent west of the Pacific Ocean. Dry land once formed a "land bridge" connecting Asia with North America. This bridge was probably how the first Native Americans traveled here.

Glossary

assembly line (a SEM blee)- a way of making a product where each worker does the same job over and over. The product moves by as it is put together.

automobile- another name for a car.

baggataway- a very popular Indian stick ball game played like lacrosse. It was a contest with two large teams. The players used sticks shaped to form a sort of racket by which the ball could be caught, carried or thrown. The ball was animal hair covered with leather. The object was to hurl the ball between goalposts set up at either end of a field.

ballot- the official form or list which tells who is running for different elected offices. It may also include issues which will be decided a vote. For example, Sally Smith's name was added to the ballot for city mayor.

bargaining (BAR gun ing)- the give and take of reaching an agreement. Deciding what each group will give and receive.

Battle Creek [Calhoun County] Population 53,500. Known as the Cereal City. Famous for making breakfast cereal. Home of the Kellogg Company. Southwest LP.

Bay City [Bay County] Population 38,900. Started as a lumber town. A busy port city. Beans are exported from here. It is known for ship building. Located on Saginaw Bay.

Benton Harbor [Berrien County] Population 12,800. Located on Lake Michigan. A twin city with St. Joseph. Home of the Whirlpool Corporation. Southwest LP.

"big wheels"- large wheels nine to ten feet tall pulled by horses. They were used to haul logs over the bumpy ground in the woods without a sled. With them lumbering could be done the year round.

bill- the official name of an idea for a new law. The law makers vote on each bill. If the bill is passed by both groups of lawmakers and signed by the governor, it will become a law.

birchbark- bark from a birch tree which can be peeled off in thin layers. It was used by the tribes to make containers, cover the wigwams and canoes. It is white on the outside and tan on the inside.

Bissell (bis el), **Anna** [1846-1934]- managed the Bissell Carpet Sweeper Company in Grand Rapids, MI. from 1889-1919. She was the first woman to be the chief executive of such a large company.

board feet- the standard way to measure lumber. A piece of wood one foot long, one foot wide, and one inch thick. A board one inch thick, one foot wide and 8 feet long has 8 board feet.

bonjour (BOn jzure)- a French word meaning "good day" or "good morning".

border- a boundary or edge of a country or state, etc.

brine- underground water which has much salt along with other dissolved chemicals. The water can be evaporated and the salt used. Sometimes the other chemicals are valuable too.

Our Michigan Adventure

Brule (broo-LAY), **Etienne** (ay-TYEN) [1592 ?-1633]- believed to be the first French explorer to reach Michigan at about 1620.

bulk cargoes- freight or goods, like wheat, iron ore, or limestone, which can be poured loose into a ship's hold. Great Lakes freighters are specially designed for this kind of freight.

Bunche, Ralph [1904-1971]- the first African American to receive the Nobel Peace Prize. He was born in Detroit.

Bunyan, Paul- an imaginary 'super-sized' lumberjack, along with his big blue ox, could do many wonderful and outlandish things.

Burt, William- discovered iron ore in the U.P. in 1844 while surveying the land.

Cadillac (KAD el ak), **Antoine** (ahn TWAHN) [1658-1730]- French explorer and fur trader who started Detroit in 1701.

Cadillac (KAD el ak), **Marie-Therese** (ma REE TEH rez) [1671-1740]- wife of Antoine, was the first French woman to start a home in Michigan. It was 1701.

Canada (KAN a dah)- the large country mostly north of Michigan.

canals (KAN als)- man-made rivers used for transportation.

canoe (CAN oo)- a small, long, narrow boat pointed at both ends; usually moved by paddles, with no rudder or sail.

capital (KAP-ih-tel)- the city where the main offices of a government are located. It is also the place where the laws are made.

capital resources- equipment (machines, computers, trucks, etc.) needed for a business.

capitol building (the capital city is spelled with an "al")- the building in which state or national lawmakers meet.

carrousel (Care ah sell)- an amusement ride similar to a merry-go-round.

Cass, Lewis [1782-1866]- governor of Michigan Territory for 18 years (1813-1831). He suggested the state motto and designed the state seal. He made land treaties with the Indians and helped explore the land.

Cassopolis (cass AH pul us) [Cass County] Population 1,800. Many escaped slaves settled here before the Civil War. Southwest LP.

CCC or **Civilian Conservation Corps** (Siv il yun Kon sir va shun Kor)- A government-run program during the Great Depression which gave jobs to thousands of unemployed young men. The men lived in camps and did outdoor work such as building roads or planting trees.

chariot (chair e ut)- A vehicle of ancient times that had two wheels and was pulled by horses. Used in the story about Henry Ford's "999" race car to mean a dangerous thing to drive.

Glossary

Chicago Road- the early road first built to carry soldiers and military supplies to go from Detroit to Fort Dearborn at Chicago. In the 1830s and 1840s it was used by many pioneers moving across Michigan. Today it is U.S. 12.

China- a country of east and central Asia. British and French explorers wanted to find a shorter route to China where they could buy trade goods, especially spices and silk. It is about 8,000 miles west of Michigan.

Chippewa- a name usually used by the British for the Ojibwa tribe.

cholera (KOL er a)- a disease which killed many people years ago. People threw up and had to go to the bathroom so much they became weak and often died.

Chrysler (KRI sler), **Walter** [1875-1940]- started the Chrysler Corporation in 1925. By 1937 his company was the No. 2 producer in the car industry.

city council- the people elected to make laws or give advice for a city.

civil rights (SIV el)- the basic rights people have so that each person is treated equally and fairly, no matter who they are.

Civil War- a war between two or more parts of the same country. The United States had a civil war (1861-1865) between the northern states which were against slavery and the southern states which were for slavery. The war started when the southern states tried to form their own country.

climate (KLY met)- weather conditions at a place, over a period of years. Shown by winds, rains, temperature, etc.

colonies (KOL eh neez)- groups of people who settle in a new country but remain under the control of their original country or king.

communicate (KUM u na kate)- the exchange of information between persons in all kinds of ways. People can communicate by speaking, using radios, telephones, e-mail, etc.

compass (KUM-pus)- a device with a magnetic needle that shows direction by pointing north.

"conductors"- people working on the Underground Railroad who took slaves from one hiding place to another.

Confederate States of America (kun fed ur et)- another name for the Confederacy; eleven southern states believing in slavery that pulled out of the United States in 1860 and 1861. They fought against the northern states in the United States Civil War.

Congress- another name for the lawmakers in Washington, D.C.

conservation (Kon sir va shun)- protecting natural resources to prevent waste or destruction.

constitution (KON stuh tu shun)- written set of rules used to govern a state or country.

consumer- a person who buys products like shoes, or services like lawn mowing.

Cooper (KOO per), **Tom** [? 1906]- a well-known bicycle racer who supplied money for Henry Ford to build his race car, the '999'. He was killed in 1906 in a car accident in New York.

Our Michigan Adventure

Copper Harbor [Keweenaw County]- on tip of the peninsula in Lake Superior. The most northern town in Michigan.

copper- a common metal that is very flexible and an excellent conductor of electricity. Copper mining was a big industry in Michigan from 1880 to 1920.

coral (KOR al)- the rock-like skeletons of various salt water forms of life which live in large clumps.

core democratic values- our government and constitution are based on these key values. Examples are liberty, justice, equality, the right to vote and religious freedom.

Cornish (KOR nish)- people from Cornwall who came to work in Michigan's mines. Cornwall is a small part of Britain.

counties (kOUn tees)- units of local government within a state. A state is divided into many counties which contain cities, villages, and townships. Most Michigan counties are shown as square boxes on maps.

county commissioners (KO mish in ners)- the elected men and women responsible for running the government of a county.

court's branch or judicial branch- the part of state government having to do with courts and judges. It is one of the three branches of government.

Couzens (KUZ zins), **James** [1872-1936]- a hard-working executive in the Ford Motor Company, quit his job in 1915 because of Henry Ford's outspoken ideas regarding World War I. He was a U.S. senator from 1922-1936. During the Great Depression he gave 10 million dollars to help needy children.

crosscut saw- a long saw, having a handle at each end, used for cutting down trees.

Cuba (KUE bah)- an island in the West Caribbean Sea, south of Florida. Some of the Hispanic people in Michigan have ancestors from Cuba.

Custer (KUSS ter), **George Armstrong** [1839-1876]- from Monroe, MI. commanded a Michigan cavalry unit during the Civil War.

customs (KUS-tems)- the usual ways of doing things among a group of people.

de Sable (day-SAW-bul), **Jean** (jHAN) [1745-1818]- born in Haiti, was one of the first black men in the Michigan territory.

de Tonty (day TAHN tee), **Anne**- mother of the first European child born in Michigan.

de troit (day twaw)- French words meaning "strait," a narrow channel or river connecting two large bodies or water. These words became the name of Michigan's largest city, Detroit, though the way the words are spoken has changed.

Dearborn [Wayne County]- Population 89,300. Home of Ford Motor Company, the Henry Ford Museum, and Greenfield Village. Southeast LP.

decompose (de kum poz)- to rot, decay or disintegrate.

deed- a written legal document with a precise description of property being bought or sold.

Glossary

degrees- the units used in latitude and longitude. The degree symbol (°) is a tiny circle which is placed next to a number. The distance measured by one degree changes for longitude depending on where the measurement is taken. In the Michigan area the distance between each degree of longitude is about 50 miles. The distance between each degree of latitude is about 70 miles. Latitude distance stays the same because these lines do not come closer together near the poles of the earth as do longitude lines.

desolation (des o lay shun)- completely wrecking anything of value or usefulness; leaving no homes or buildings standing; destroying all crops and animals.

destruction (des truck shun)- the act of destroying, ruining, wrecking.

Detroit (dee TROY t) [Wayne County]- Population 1,028,000. Michigan's largest city. Started by the French in 1701. Is a neighbor city to Windsor, Canada, which is across the Detroit River. Southeast LP.

Dewey (DOO ee), **Thomas E.** [1902-1971]- born in Owosso, MI. was the Republican candidate in 1944 and 1948 for president of the U.S.

discrimination (dis krim eh NAY shun)- treating someone unfairly because of the person's difference from other people, such as race, sex, religion, size, or ability.

Dodge, Horace [1868-1920]- mechanical genius who worked closely with his brother John in supplying machine parts for the Ford Motor Company.

Dodge, John [1864-1920]- with his brother Horace started in 1914 the Dodge Motor Car Company where they made the first all-steel bodied car.

Dow, Herbert [1866-1930]- started the Dow Chemical Company in 1897 in Midland, Michigan. Now Dow is the second largest U.S. chemical company.

Durant (DUR ant), **William** (Billy) [1861-1947]- In 1886 he started a Flint, MI. company which made two-wheeled and four-wheeled buggies. In 1908 he started General Motors which became one of the world's largest companies.

Dutch (DUT ch)- the people of the country of the Netherlands, also called Holland.

Edison (ed i son), **Thomas** [1847-1931]- a great inventor who spent part of his boyhood at Port Huron, MI. and invented an electric battery there. He invented the electric light bulb and the phonograph, and hundreds of other inventions that changed the way the world lives.

election- the process of voting on issues or people for political office. Elections are held for governor, mayor, lawmakers, judges, etc.

entrepreneur (an treh pri newer)- the person who takes risks to start and manage a new business. Henry Ford was an entrepreneur when he began his car business.

equal rights- having the same rights. It does not matter if a person is a man or a woman. It does not matter about his or her race or religion. Equality.

equator (e quay tur)- an imaginary circle around the middle of the earth which is halfway between the North Pole and South Pole. The hottest part of the earth.

257

Our Michigan Adventure

Erie Canal (EAR re KAN al)- a 363 mile long man-made river connecting Albany, New York with Lake Erie. The Erie Canal opened in 1825. Many pioneers came to Michigan using this canal in the 1830s. People and freight could come to Albany from New York City using the Hudson River.

Escanaba (ES can aba) [Delta County] Population 13,700. A lumber and iron ore port on Lake Michigan. The Upper Peninsula State Fair is held here every August. South central UP.

Etherage (eth er idge), **Annie** [1840 ?]- lived during her childhood in Wisconsin where she also married. Her family returned to Detroit, MI and during a visit there Annie joined the Second Michigan Regiment as a Civil War nurse.

ethnic groups- those based on race or place of origin. Each group has similar customs and beliefs.

Europe (YOUR up)- the continent which is across the Atlantic Ocean from North America. It has the countries of Britain, Finland, France, Germany, Italy, Netherlands, Norway, Poland, Sweden, and others.

Europeans- the people who live in, or have ancestors from, the countries of Europe.

executive branch- one of the three main parts of state government. The governor is the head of this branch.

experiment- the process of carefully studying a scientific event to understand what is happening. Thomas Edison did many experiments to learn how to make a light bulb which would work.

exploration- looking for or discovering new places. Long ago people explored the earth. Now they explore the ocean and outer space.

exports- items made or grown in the United States which are taken to other countries to be sold.

Fayette (fay ET) [Delta County]- Located on Big Bay De Noc which is a part of Lake Michigan. Fayette is a ghost town left from the early iron mining days. Iron ore was brought here by ship then melted and processed. South central UP.

federal government- having to do with the national government in Washington, D.C.

ferries- boats carrying people, cars, and trucks over water.

Finland- a country in northern Europe between Sweden and Russia.

Finnish (fin ish)- something connected to or relative to the people of Finland or their language.

fireman- The person on a train engine who shoveled the wood or coal into the fire. The fire made steam to run the train.

Glossary

Flint [Genesee County] Population 140,700. Birthplace of General Motors. Known for the making of wagons and buggies before cars were invented. Southeast LP.

Ford, Gerald [1913-]- became the 38th President of the United States in 1974. He is the only person from Michigan to have that position. The Gerald Ford Museum is in Grand Rapids.

Ford, Henry [1863-1947]- In 1903 he started the Ford Motor Company. He helped start the moving assembly line for factories that made cars more affordable. His wages for auto workers brought about minimum wages in the car industry.

Fort Malden (Canada)- a British fort located in Canada at Amherstburg on the edge of the Detroit river. It was a frontier post in the War of 1812.

Fort Michilimackinac (MISH ill eh MACK in aw)- the fort built by the French at the tip of the lower peninsula in 1715. It was a fur trading center for many years. Located at the Straits in Mackinaw City. The fort has been rebuilt and is run by the state government as a tourist stop.

Fort Wilkins [Keweenaw County] A fort built at Copper Harbor in the Keweenaw Peninsula in 1844. The fort closed in 1846. Now it is a tourist stop.

Fox River- the river that Father Marquette followed in his explorations. It flows into Green Bay, Wisconsin from the middle of the state.

France- a country in western Europe, having the English Channel to the north and Spain to the south.

Frankenmuth (FRAY kin mooth) [Saginaw County] Population 4,400. Famous tourist attraction built like a German village. Home of Bronner's Christmas Wonderland. Southeast LP.

freighter (fray tur)- a ship used to carry goods or cargo, such as cars, coal, cement, etc.

Fremont [Newaygo County] Population 3,800. Known for the making of baby food. West central LP.

French- having something to do with the country, the people, or the language of France.

French and Indian War- between 1754 and 1760 the British attacked the French areas of North America and finally beat them. The Indians or Native Americans helped the French side. The French lost the war and had to leave most parts of North America.

fruit belt- land in the Lower Peninsula, along the coast of Lake Michigan, that is ideal for growing fruit.

fugitive (FEW ja tiv)- a person who is running away.

fugitive slave laws- national laws that made it a crime for anyone to help escaped slaves (fugitives). Under these laws someone helping an escaped slave could be fined or put into prison.

Genesee County (jin eh see)- City of Flint located here. The area is known for making cars and car parts. Southeast LP.

German (JER men)- having something to do with the country, the people, or the language of Germany.

Germany (JER man ee)- a country in central Europe. More people in Michigan have ancestors from this country than any other country.

glacier (GLAY sher)- a very thick ice sheet which slowly covers a wide area of land because more snow falls in the winter than can melt in the summer.

global positioning (GLOW bull po zish on ing)- using information from a satellite to give a very accurate location. The location is given in degrees of latitude and longitude.

Gordy, Berry [1929-]- started Motown as a Detroit record company in 1959 which became one of the most successful black businesses in the United States.

government (state, federal or national)- the system which rules a country, state, or city. It makes the laws, collects taxes, operates the courts, police, military forces and so forth.

governor's branch or executive branch (eg-ZEK-eh-tiv)- one of the three parts of government. The president and governor are in this branch.

Grand Rapids [Kent County] Population 189,100. Has been called the Furniture City. Is the second largest city in Michigan. Located on the Grand River. Central LP.

Grand River- Michigan's longest river. It starts in Hillsdale County and flows through Lansing and Grand Rapids into Lake Michigan.

Great Depression (dee PRESH en)- the years from 1929 until about 1939 when there was a great business slowdown; banks closed; companies went out of business, and many people could not get jobs.

Great Lakes Region (REE jun)- the land touching any of the five Great Lakes. It usually includes Michigan, Ohio, Wisconsin, Minnesota, Illinois, and Indiana. Sometimes New York, Pennsylvania and Ontario, Canada are included too.

Griffon- a make-believe animal with the body of a lion and wings of an eagle. A carved griffon was placed on the bow of La Salle's ship which was named the *Griffon*. Sometimes spelled *Griffin*.

Haviland, Laura [1807-1898]- located in Lenawee county she and her husband had one of the first U.S. schools to admit black children. She helped thousands of escaped slaves through the Underground Railroad to Canada.

headquarters- the main office of a business.

heritage (HAIR uh tij)- something handed down from ancestors or relatives. Often customs, ideas, or traditions from your ancestors which you still follow.

Glossary

Hiawatha (HI eh WA tha)- name given to an Indian in legends. His name was made famous in a poem written by Henry Wadsworth Longfellow. The name means "he makes rivers".

Hispanic (HISS pan ik)- the prefix "his" of the word Hispanic means *relating to*. In this case Hispanic means relating to Spain. Hispanic people are those from Central and South America which were once controlled by Spain. People from Mexico, Puerto Rico, Cuba, etc. are often called Hispanic.

Holland [Ottawa County] Population 30,700. Settled by Dutch immigrants. City has the world famous Tulip Time Festival for a week each May. West central LP.

Holland also **Netherlands-** a small country in northwest Europe. Some people from this country moved to western Michigan around the cities of Grand Rapids, Holland, and Zeeland.

Houghton(HO tun), **Douglass** [1809-1845]- Michigan's first state geologist, reported large copper deposits in the U.P. This started the copper industry in the 1800s.

Houghton [Houghton County] Population 7,500. In the former copper mining region. Located at the base of the Keweenaw Peninsula.

Houghton Lake (HO tun)- Michigan's largest inland lake. The home of Tip-Up-Town USA festival each winter. It is the scene of many winter sports. In Roscommon county North central LP.

Hull, William [1753-1825]- first governor of the Michigan Territory from 1805-1812. Following the War of 1812 he was court-martialed and sentenced to be shot for his quick surrender of Detroit. President Madison, however, considered his previous bravery and gave him a pardon.

human resources- the people who provide their skill and energy to run or manage a business.

Huron (hYOUR on)- or **Wyandotte** (WY-n-dot)- one of the smaller tribes living in Michigan. They were located along the southeastern coast of the Lower Peninsula.

Illinois (ILL in noy)- an Indian tribe who lived in the state which was named after them. They spoke a language similar to that of some Michigan tribes.

immigrants (IM a grents)- people who come from one country to live in another country.

immigrate (em IH great)- to move into another country to live.

imports- products or food from another country which are shipped to the United States and sold.

income tax- money paid to a government based on how much a person earns.

independence- freedom of control by others; self-government.

Indiana (IN dee AN ah)- a north central state of the U.S. located south of Michigan and east of Illinois. It became a state in 1816.

interstate highways (I-75, I-94, etc.)- limited access highways that cross state lines. They go from one state to another. Interstates usually have at least two lanes going each way.

invention- a break through or new idea to make something useful. Thomas Edison invented main types of the record player, motion pictures (movies), and the electric light.

invest- to put money into a business to help it grow with the hope of making a profit. Businesses need investors to provide the money to get started, to buy equipment, raw materials, and to pay the first wages, etc.

investors- people who put money in a business in order to make more money; people who buy stock in a company.

Ireland (I er land)- an island nation near Britain. Many people came from Ireland to the United State and Michigan to find a better life.

Irish (I rish)- of or relating to Ireland, its people or its language.

iron- a heavy metal which is attracted by magnets. It is used to make steel. Iron is mined in the Upper Peninsula.

Iron Mountain- [Dickinson County] Population 8,500. Rich iron deposits were found here in 1879. Located near the Wisconsin border. South central UP.

Ironwood [Gogebic County] Population 6,800. Is farther west than any Michigan city. It borders on the State of Wisconsin. Northwest UP.

Iroquois (EAR a kwoi)- a group of Native American (Indian) tribes who lived south of Lake Ontario. They were very warlike and powerful. They were among the first tribes to get guns from the Europeans.

Isle Royale (eyel roy ul)- A national park. It is the largest island in Lake Superior. Known for the wolves and moose who live there. Once had a fishing industry and copper mines.

Italians (IT tal yuns)- people who were born or have ancestors in Italy, a country in southern Europe.

Italy (it eh LEE)- a country in southern Europe in the Mediterranean Sea. It is shaped like a boot on maps. A few of the first Europeans to come to Michigan were from Italy.

Jackson [Jackson County] Population 37,400. The Republican Party was started here. Michigan's largest prison is nearby. South central LP.

Japanese (Jap eh nees)- people born or living in Japan, an island country in the western Pacific Ocean, located off the east coast of Asia.

job security- knowing that you will keep your job if you do good work. Not worrying about being fired from your job for some small mistake or disagreement.

Johnston, Susan [1776-1843]- a Native American woman who helped obtain the 1820 land treaty for the U.S. government from the Ojibwa.

Glossary

Jolliet (ZHOL ee ay), **Louis** (loo ee) [1645-1700]-French explorer of the Mississippi River and Great Lakes region.

judicial branch- one of the three main parts of state government. This branch has the courts. It gets it name from the judges who are in charge of the courts.

jury- people who decide who is right in a trial. Some juries have 12 people, others have fewer members.

Kalamazoo (kal ah mah zoo) [Kalamazoo County] Population 80,300. Home of Western Michigan University and Kalamazoo College. Southwest LP.

Kalkaska (sounds like- kal KAS ka) [Kalkaska County] Population 1,900. Home of the National Trout Festival each spring. The state soil is named after Kalkaska and is found in this area. Northwest LP.

Kawbawgam (kaw baw gam), **Charlotte** (SHAR lot) [1832-1904]- sued the Jackson Mining Company for the rights given to her father, a Chippewa chief. The rights were finally given to her.

Kellogg, Dr. Harvey [1852-1943]- head of a large sanitarium in Battle Creek in 1876 where he developed granola as a health food. His brother, William K. Kellogg, later patented and sold breakfast cereal based on Harvey's ideas.

Kellogg, Will [1850-1951]- in 1906 started the Battle Creek Toasted Corn Flake Company. The Kellogg Company continues to make breakfast cereal today.

Kentucky (ken TUK ee)- an east central state in the United States, south of Indiana and Ohio and west of West Virginia. It was settled before Michigan and became a state in 1792.

Keweenaw Peninsula (KEY wa naw)- Northern most point of Michigan which extends into Lake Superior. An area of very heavy snowfall in the winter. Northwest UP.

La Salle (lah sal), **Robert** [1643-1687]- French explorer who built Fort Miami, the first French fort in Michigan, where St. Joseph, MI. is today. He also built the *Griffon*, first large sailing boat to sail on the Great Lakes.

labor unions- groups formed by workers to get better working conditions and wages.

land office- a government office where the sale of land owned by the government is recorded. Settlers went to the land office to buy their land during pioneer days.

Lansing (lan sing) [Ingham County] Population 127,300. Is Michigan's State Capitol. The capital was moved there in 1848. Is located near the center of the LP.

Latin (LAT n)- an ancient language sometimes used for the words of a motto, as in the Michigan motto. The Romans spoke Latin 2,000 years ago.

latitude (LAT eh tude)- lines on a map or globe that measure distance in degrees (°) north or south of the equator. Latitude and longitude lines are used together by navigators and surveyors to find exact places.

lava (LAH vah)- melted rock coming from a volcano.

lawmaker's branch or legislative branch- the part of a government that makes laws. It is divided into a house of representatives and a senate. Both parts must pass the same bill before it can become a law.

lawmakers or legislators- men and women who are elected to make laws.

laws- official rules to live by. There are penalties for not obeying laws.

legend (leh jend)- a widely told story which is often make-believe.

legislative branch- one of the three main branches of state government. This is the branch which makes the laws. It is divided into two parts. One part is called the house of representatives and the other is the senate.

legislature (LED jus lay ture)- a group of elected people who have the power to make, change, or cancel laws.

limestone- a soft rock, like chalk, which came from sea shells. It is used to make cement and to process iron into steel. It is often moved by ship on the Great Lakes.

Lindbergh, Charles (LIND berg) [1902-1974]- a famous early pilot who was born in Detroit. He was the first person to fly alone across the Atlantic Ocean. He worked in Michigan for a short time in World War II, but spent most of his life outside of the state.

litterbug (a person)- a slang term for someone who carelessly throws trash and rubbish on the ground or in the water.

locks- like a canal but with gates at each end. Water flows in or out to raise or lower ships as they pass from higher or lower lakes or oceans.

log jam- a pile of logs on the way to a sawmill which become stuck in a river.

log mark- a mark stamped on the end of logs to show to whom they belong.

"Lone Ranger"- the name of a radio program first introduced by radio station WXYZ in Detroit. Its star was a masked man who rode a horse called Silver. The program was on the air from 1932 to 1954. Later it became a television program.

longhouse- a long Native American lodge or home covered with sheets of bark. The length and width depended on the number of families living inside. In Michigan longhouses were used mostly by the Hurons.

longitude (LON ji tude)- a way to find distance on the earth going east and west. A city in England is the starting point or 0°. The lines which go up and down on a map or globe.

Louis, Joe [1914-1981]- grew up in Detroit and was world heavyweight boxing champion from 1937 to 1949. Detroit's sports arena is named in his honor.

Lower Peninsula (pe nin se la)- the southern part of Michigan where nearly nine million people live. It is shaped like a mitten on the map.

lumberjacks- men who cut down trees and prepared the logs for the sawmill. They were also called shanty boys because they lived in simple cabins or shanties.

Mackinac Island (MACK in aw EYE land)- a small island in Lake Huron. It was a fur trading center during the 1700s and early 1800s. Today it is a popular tourist stop. Thousands of people visit it each summer, but only a few hundred stay in the winter.

Glossary

Macomb County (MAH kom)- borders Lake St. Clair and St. Clair River in southeastern Michigan. It has the third highest population of any county in the state. Named after General Alexander Macomb who was a hero from the War of 1812.

maize- a kind of corn with a smaller ear and smaller kernels that was an important Native American food.

malaria (ma-LAIR-ee-eh)- a sickness caused by the bite of one kind of mosquito. It brings on a bad fever and chills. Early settlers called it "ague" (A gyou).

Malcolm X [1925-1965]- his real name was Malcolm Little. He grew up in Lansing, MI. During the 1960s there were strong civil rights movements. As Malcolm X he believed in militant methods and became a leader in the Black Muslim movement. His work ended in 1965 when he was shot and killed.

Manistee (MAN es tee) [Manistee County] Population 6,700. Began as the site of a saw-mill in 1841. It is said to mean "spirit of the woods." Located on Lake Michigan. LP.

manufacture- the process of making products for sale. For example, the car was manu-factured in Warren, Michigan.

Marquette (mar KETT), **Jacques** (jHAK) [1637-1675]- French missionary who started the city of Sault Ste. Marie in 1668 and then St. Ignace in 1671. With Jolliet in 1673 he explored the Mississippi River. Marquette died in 1675 near Ludington, MI. He was buried near a river which is named the Pere Marquette River.

Marquette (mar-KETT)- [Marquette County] - county has more land than any in Michi-gan. Also home to the city of Marquette which is an important iron loading port on Lake Superior. The city is the largest in the Upper Peninsula. Population about 22,000.

Marshall [Calhoun County] Population 6,900. A city with many historic homes. It was once thought the capital would be moved there. Located between Jackson and Battle Creek. LP.

Mason, Stevens T. [1811-1843]- Michigan's first state governor, was known as the 'Boy Governor' since he was only twenty-three years old. He was governor until 1840.

mayor- the chief official of a city; the head of city government.

McCoy (mick koy), **Elijah** (ee lie ja) [1844-1929]- a black inventor born to fugitive slaves living in Canada. He is famous for his automatic lubricating cup which oiled the train wheels while the train was moving. The engineer did not have to stop and oil the wheels.

Menominee [Menominee County] Population 9,400. Borders Wisconsin and Green Bay.

Menominee River (meh NOM eh nee)- much used in logging days. It flows into Lake Michigan. Forms part of the border between Michigan and Wisconsin.

Menominee tribe (meh NOM eh nee)- this tribe lived in the middle part of the Upper Peninsula. The Menominee River is named for them. Their name is an Ojibwa word for "wild rice people." Wild rice was an important food for them. Their customs were much like those of the Ojibwa who lived nearby.

Mexico (MEX eh ko)- the large country located south of the United States. Many Hispanic people come from Mexico to the United States and Michigan.

Miami- This tribe lived in the Lower Peninsula near Niles. Their tribe did not have many people and their area did not include much of Michigan.

Midland [Midland County] Population 38,000. Home of Dow Chemical Company. Much salt water brine is under the land in this area. Near Saginaw Bay. Northeast LP.

migrate (MY grate)- when many people move from one area to another.

mine- usually one or more underground tunnels where a mineral is dug out and moved to the surface.

minerals- natural materials which are useful or valuable. Copper, gold, iron ore, oil, limestone, and salt are all minerals.

missionaries (MISH un air rees)- people who go to other countries or areas to teach about their religion.

Mississippi River (Miss-eh-SIP-ee)- the longest river in the United States. It starts in Minnesota and flows mostly south until it reaches the Gulf of Mexico. Marquette and Jolliet first explored the upper part of this river.

Model T- the car which Henry Ford first made in 1908. It became one of the most popular, most affordable, and easiest to repair cars in America. It was made from 1908 until 1927 with over 15 million sold.

Monroe (MUN row) [Monroe County] Population 22,900. Most southeastern city in the state and the one with the lowest elevation.

Montreal- A large city in Canada along the St. Lawrence River. In the fur trading days, many furs were shipped from Michigan to Montreal.

motor vehicles- a name given to any vehicle powered by an engine or motor. Cars, buses, and trucks are motor vehicles.

Motown (MO town)- not a real place. Short for "motor town." It is a nickname for Detroit.

motto (MOT-toe)- a short statement that says what someone believes or what something stands for. It is a custom that some mottoes are written in Latin.

Mt. Arvon (Mt. stands for mount, like mountain)- The highest point in Michigan at 1,979 feet above sea level. It is in the north central UP.

Mt. Curwood- A mountain in the north central UP which is only a few feet lower than Mt. Arvon. The two mountain are not far apart.

Mt. Pleasant [Isabella County] Population 23,300. Home of Central Michigan University. A tribal reservation is nearby. Located in central part of the Lower Peninsula.

Muskegon (mus KEE gon) [Muskegon County]- Population 40,300. Started as a lumber town and became a busy port city. Once called the "Lumber Queen of the World." The famous Charles Hackley mansion is here. The World War II submarine *Silversides* can be visited.

Glossary

Muslim religion (MUZ lem)- the religious faith established by Mohammed in the Mid-East (the Arabic lands overseas).

national government- the government based in Washington, D.C. It governs the nation. Sometimes called the federal government. The President of the United States is the head of the national government.

Native Americans- a term used to name the first people of the United States; the Indians. The word native means first or pure.

natural resources- the raw materials in nature such as metal, trees, water, etc., that may be used by people to make something useful.

Nazi- a member of a German political party (1933-1945) opposing human rights, and especially against Jews and Blacks.

negotiator (NEE go she a tor)- a person who helps two or more groups settle their differences. They might help make a treaty and so forth.

New France- a French colony (1609 to 1763) in North America which included Michigan and Canada.

New York state- a middle Atlantic state in the U.S. located south of Lake Ontario. It reaches from the Atlantic Ocean to Lake Erie.

Niagara Falls (NI ag are uh)- falls of the Niagara River on the United States-Canada border where water from Lake Erie falls 161 feet into Lake Ontario on its way to the Atlantic Ocean.

nicknames- Michigan has several nicknames. Three of these are the Great Lakes State because Michigan is surrounded by the Great Lakes. Water Wonderland because we have the Great Lakes and many beautiful inland lakes. Wolverine State because the people from Ohio felt we were being mean and nasty in the argument over the border in 1835.

Nobel Peace Prize (no-BEL)- an award given each year to honor men and women who work to make life better for others. Alfred Nobel was a rich inventor who left all his money for this prize.

nominee- a person selected by a political party to run for political office.

North America- the land containing the countries of Mexico, United States, and Canada.

North Pole- the most northern part of the earth. The top of the earth as shown on a map or globe.

Northwest Territory- A former United States frontier area that included the present states of Illinois, Indiana, Michigan, Ohio, Wisconsin, and part of Minnesota. It was formed in 1787.

Norway- a country in northwestern Europe, bordered by the Atlantic Ocean on the west and by Sweden to the east.

Oakland County- The county with the second most people in Michigan. Located north of Detroit. Southeastern Lower Peninsula.

Ohio (OH hi oh)- a north central state south of Michigan and Lake Erie. Ohio became a state before Michigan in 1803. A disagreement in 1835 between the people of Michigan and those of Ohio over the location of the border between them resulted in what is called "The Toledo War".

oil- a thick dark liquid which is pumped from under the ground. It burns and is made into diesel fuel, gasoline and fuel oil for furnaces.

Ojibwa (o JIB wah)- A large tribe which does not just live in Michigan. They are found all across the northern Great Lakes area. Probably the largest tribe living in Michigan. They shared the Upper Peninsula with the Menominee.

Oldfield, Barney- a bicycle racer from Toledo, Ohio who lived to go fast. He probably did not know how to drive before he practiced with the 999 race car. He went on to become a famous race car driver.

Olds, Ransom [1864-1950]- started the first Michigan automobile company in 1897. In 1901 he moved the company to Lansing. He left that company in 1904, however, and started one called REO (after his own initials). After 1907 he faded away from the auto industry. He died in 1950. Even his mansion in Lansing was torn down to make room for a freeway.

opportunity- a chance to do something or get something you want or need. Most opportunities have trade offs. For example, Thomas had an opportunity to enter the contest but he would need to skip the basketball game to do it.

ordinance (OR din anse)- another name for a law. The Northwest Ordinance of 1787 is an example.

ore (OR)- a mineral which is not a pure metal. It must be refined to obtain the metal.

Ottawa (OT ah wah) or Odawa. A tribe of the northwest Lower Peninsula. The Ojibwa and Ottawa were related. Many of their ways of living and doing things were also alike.

Owosso (oh WA so) [Shiawassee County] Population 16,300. Birthplace of Thomas E. Dewey who ran for president in 1944 and 1948. Located Northeast of Lansing.

paces- measurements determined by the length of a step in walking; usually 2.5 feet equals one pace.

passenger pigeon (pas in jer pij jun)- a North American wild pigeon. At one time there were millions of this bird, but it was hunted so much that it is now extinct. Huge flocks once flew over Michigan.

pasty (PASS tee)- a meat pie including potatoes, turnips, and onions. It was considered the "box lunch" for Cornish miners.

patent- the official rights given by the government to the first person to invent something. This allows the inventor to be the only one to make the invention for 17 years.

Glossary

Pearl Harbor, Hawaii- An island far away in the Pacific Ocean. It is the location of the surprise attack on the U.S. Navy by Japanese planes. This event occurred on December 7, 1941.

peninsula- a piece of land which has water around it on three sides. A piece of land sticking out into a lake or ocean.

Perry, Oliver Hazard [1785-1819]- American naval officer who fought the British in the battle of Lake Erie during the War of 1812. After the battle he sent his famous victory message: "We have met the enemy and they are ours."

Petoskey [Emmet County] Population 6,100. Known as the area where the state stone can be found along beaches. A scenic tourist spot. On Lake Michigan near top of lower Peninsula.

Ph. D.- an abbreviation for doctor of philosophy. It is usually used for professors at colleges. Men and women who went to medical school are not usually called Ph. D. s

pioneer- someone who moved to a place in the early days. An early settler. The words *pioneer* and *settler* are often both used to mean the same people. Someone who came to Michigan in the late 1700s or early 1800s.

plank road- an early kind of road made by laying down wooden boards or planks. They were not very satisfactory and soon rotted.

plow- a piece of farm equipment used to break up, lift, or turn over the soil.

Polish (POLE esh)- referring to the people or the language of Poland, a country in central Europe.

political party (poll-LIT-i-kel)- a group of people with similar ideas who work to have certain persons elected to government offices. The two main political parties in the United States are the Republican Party and the Democratic Party.

pollution (po LU shun)- damage to the environment caused by poisonous or toxic materials, waste, garbage, or junk.

Pontiac (PON tee ak), Chief [1720-1769]—an Ottawa leader who was probably born near the Maumee River in Ohio. He helped the tribes try to drive the British out of the Great Lakes Region in 1763. He organized the longest attack by Native Americans on a fort (Detroit). Later, he left the Michigan area. He was murdered by other Indians near St. Louis Missouri in 1769.

Pontiac [Oakland County] Population 71,200. Named after the Indian chief. The Silverdome is located near here. North of Detroit in southeast LP.

population (pop u lay sun)- the number of people living in a city or state, etc. The population of Michigan is about nine million people.

Port Huron [St. Clair County] Population 33,700. Has Blue Water Bridge across the St. Clair River to Canada. Is further east than any other city in Lower Peninsula. Boyhood home of Thomas Edison between 1854 and the mid 1860s.

portage (POR tej)- a short distance on land which has to be crossed between two rivers or lakes by those traveling by boat or canoe.

ports- cities with harbors next to large rivers, lakes or oceans where ships load and unload.

Posen (POE sen) [Presque Isle County]- Population 263. Town south of Rogers City near Lake Huron.

Potawatomi (POT a WAT o me)- The Potawatomi settled in southern Michigan by the 1750s. The Potawatomi name comes from Ojibwa words for fire. They probably got this name because they burned the grassland before planting their crops.

priests (preests)- ministers and religious leaders, often in the Catholic Church.

producer- the person or business who makes a product or service. Nike produces shoes.

property tax- money that is charged to the owner of land or buildings to pay for local government and schools each year.

public service- a service provided by a government. State parks are a public service by the state of Michigan. Police protection is a public service of most cities.

Puerto Rico (PWHERE toe REE ko)- a self-governing island associated with the United States. It is in the Atlantic Ocean near Cuba.

quarry (KWOR-ree)- a large open pit usually for mining stone, limestone or gravel.

Quebec (KAY bek)- a city on the St. Lawrence River in Canada. During the 1700s the French had a large, important fort there. Also a province (like a state) of Canada where most of the people speak French and have French customs.

racial injustice (RAY shul in JUS tiss)- the violation of another person's rights because of his or her race. Not letting someone of another race get a job, buy a home or go to certain schools.

rapids- part of a river where the water flows very fast, sometimes over rocks often causing the water to foam. It can be difficult or impossible for boats to go through rapids without being wrecked.

ration (RASH en)- In World War II the government limited the amount of food, gasoline, and other things such as shoes which civilians could buy. They did this so the military would have the supplies needed to fight the war.

raw materials- materials needed to make a product. Wood is a raw material needed to make furniture.

recycling- to treat or process something so it may be used again.

region (REE jun)- any large area having similar geography or features such as mountains, lakes or a desert.

religion (REE lidg un)- a belief in God or a supreme spiritual being; a system of faith and worship.

religious freedom (ree lij us)- the right to practice the religion of choice without interference from the government or other individuals.

Glossary

Republican Party (ree-PUB-li-ken)- one of the two main political parties in the United States. It was first started to be against slavery. This party usually believes it is best to have less governmental control of people. Their first large meeting was in Jackson, Michigan in 1854.

research (ree serch)-careful scientific study and investigation to discover or explain something. The effort to invent something. The Wright brothers spent much time researching how to build an airplane.

reservation (REZ er vay shun)- land set aside by the U.S. government as a place where Native Americans can live.

resort (re zort)- a place where people go for a vacation.

Reuther (ROO ther), **Walter** [1907-1970]- came to Detroit in 1927 to try his luck in the car industry. He and his brothers Roy and Victor were active in the labor unions. Walter was leader of the United Auto Workers Union for many years. In May 1970 he and his wife died in the tragic crash of a small plane.

revolution (rev-o-LU-shen)- people rise up and change their government by force.

riot (rEYE ot)- when a large number of people become violent, out of control, and create a disturbance or confusion. Some riots are over political issues.

river hogs- the lumbermen who balanced themselves on top of the logs as they floated down the rivers. These men kept the logs from piling up into a log jam.

Saginaw (SAG en aw) [Saginaw County] Population 69,500. On Saginaw River. Was once a busy lumbering center. Located near Saginaw Bay. Lower Peninsula.

sales tax- an amount of money added on to the price of products (except food and medicine) and must be paid when the products are bought.

sap- the liquid that circulates through a tree or plant. Maple syrup is made from the sap of maple trees.

Saran Wrap (sah RAN rap)- the thin, clear, plastic wrap invented by Dow Chemical. It contains chlorine which can come from brine.

Saudi Arabia (SAW dee ah RAY be ah)- a wealthy kingdom on the Arabian Peninsula. It supplies oil to much of the world.

Sauk (sawk)- a tribe from long ago which lived in the middle Lower Peninsula area. Saginaw is said to mean place of the Sauk. They seem to have often had fights with nearby tribes. The Sauk had mostly disappeared from the state by the 1800s.

Sault Ste. Marie (soo SAYnt MAR ee)- Population 14,700. The Upper Peninsula city with the Soo Locks, the world's busiest locks. Across the river from the Canadian city with the same name. (between Lake Superior and Lake Huron). Northeastern UP.

sauna (SAW nah)- a steam bath where water is thrown on heated stones. It was invented by the Finnish people.

sawmill- a building where machines saw logs into boards and lumber.

scarce- something hard to find or in short supply.

scarcity (scare sit tee)- refers to anything that is in short supply or difficult to get. There is often a scarcity of time and money to do new projects.

Scotch- refers to the language, people, or culture of the country of Scotland which is a land in northern Britain. Scotland was conquered by the British in the 1700s.

sea lamprey (SEE lam prey)- an eel-like animal which feeds off fish by sucking their blood

segregation (seg re GAY shun)- when people are forced into separate groups often based on race.

self-sufficient- able to get along without help from others.

settlements- small villages started by pioneers which grew to be our cities of today.

settler- a pioneer. Someone who comes to start a home or farm when the land is a wilderness .

shanty boy- another name for lumberjack or logger. A shanty is a shack.

Shaw, Anna Howard [1847-1919]- from Big Rapids, worked for the voting rights of women, receiving national honors.

Shelley, Rebecca [1887-1984]- of Battle Creek, was a believer in peace with strong feelings against war.

shield (as a highway label)- the shape on which highway numbers are printed. The same shape shield will be used for all of the same kind of highways on a map.

silk- a fine, soft thread made by silkworms.

sit-down strike- takes place when workers stop the operation of a plant or factory. The workers sit down and refuse to leave. This is designed to force the employer to bargain with the workers for better pay or working conditions.

slave catchers- people who received money for capturing and returning runaway slaves to their masters.

slavery (SLA-ver-ee)- the custom where certain people own other people. The slaves are forced to do hard work without any pay. Slaves were bought and sold without their permission. Their families were broken up and taken away.

snow shoe- a light wooden frame with strips of leather stretched across it. Invented by Native Americans and used to help them walk over deep, soft snow.

snow snake- a game played by children of the Ojibwa tribe. Each player sees who can slide a long smooth stick the farthest in the snow.

Soo Locks- a system which raises and lowers ships. It goes between Lake Superior and Lake Huron. It is needed because Lake Superior is about 20 feet higher than Huron.

soul- the spiritual part of a person.

spices- something that adds flavor to food; seasoning.

Glossary

St. Ignace (SAYnt IG ness) [Mackinac County] Population 2,600. Was one of the first settlements in Michigan. Located at the straits of Mackinac in the Upper Peninsula.

St. Joseph River (SAYnt JOE sif)- It flows from Hillsdale County into Lake Michigan.

St. Lawrence River (Lawrence sounds like LOR ents)- Water from the Great Lakes flows through this river into the Atlantic Ocean.

St. Mary's River. Separates Michigan and Canada—is between Lake Huron and Lake Superior. The Soo Locks take ships around the fast rapids in this river.

stagecoach- a coach pulled by horses. It carried passengers and parcels over a regular route. Used mostly in this country from the 1790s to 1850s.

state house of representatives (reh pri zen tah tivs)- the elected officials who make up one-half of our lawmakers. They represent smaller districts than the senate. There are 110 state representatives and they are elected for two-year terms.

state senate- refers to the other half of the elected officials who make up our lawmakers. Senate districts are larger and have more people than those in the house of representatives. There are 38 state senators and they are elected for four-year terms.

state symbols- objects or living things that represent our state.

Steinman (STINE man), **Dr. David** [1887- 1961]- a famous designer of bridges. He designed "Big Mac", the Mackinac Bridge which connects Michigan's Upper and Lower Peninsulas. The bridge opened in 1957.

stock- a legal paper showing part ownership in a company. Stock is usually divided into a certain number of shares. For example, Sue owns 200 shares of stock in General Motors.

stock market- a place where shares of stock in companies are bought and sold.

stock market crash- A selling panic causing the sudden fall in the value of stock. A time when many people wish to sell their stock and no one wants to buy.

Stone, Lucinda [1814-1900]- of Kalamazoo, worked for the voting rights of Michigan women. She and her husband started in 1843 what is now Kalamazoo College.

straits (strates)- narrow waterways connecting two lakes or oceans. The Straits of Mackinac separate the Upper and Lower Peninsula. Detroit is on a strait between Lake St. Clair and Lake Erie.

Straits of Mackinac (MACK-in-aw)- Located between the Upper and Lower Peninsulas of Michigan. These straits connect Lake Michigan and Lake Huron.

strike- when all or almost all workers stop or refuse to work unless given better pay, shorter hours, or some other demand.

suburbs- cities and towns just outside a very large city. At first people move to the suburb to get away from the crowds of the city, but soon most suburbs become just as crowded.

succotash (SUC o tash)- a Native American dish made of lima beans and corn cooked together.

Our Michigan Adventure

sugar beets- a large beet with a white or light tan root which has a sweet juice that can be made into sugar.

supply of money- the amount of money and credit that is available for people to use and borrow. If the supply of money falls, it hurts business.

supreme court- (sue-PREEM)- the highest court. Each state has one and so does the United States. The state courts are for cases about state law.

surveyors (sir-VA-ers)- people who measure land and make a record of the measurements. Surveyors help people know where their land is located and where their neighbor's land starts.

Sweden (SWEE den)- a country in northwest Europe. It is part of a peninsula. It is bordered on the west by Norway, and on the east by Finland.

Swedish (SWEE dish)- refers to the people, language, and culture of Sweden.

taconite (TAK on eyet)- the name for the little marbles of iron ore which are used today. It is easier to ship the ore as taconite to the steel mills.

Tahquamenon Falls (tah-KWAH-meh-non)- One of the most beautiful falls in eastern United States. Located in the Upper Peninsula west of Sault Ste Marie.

tart cherries- a favorite fruit from Michigan's fruit belt, especially the area of Traverse City. Michigan is the largest producer of red tart cherries in the United States. This is the kind of cherry used to make pies.

taxes- the money that people and businesses pay to run the government. Taxes pay for the salary of government workers and supplies. They pay for roads and schools, etc.

Tecumseh (Ta KUM see) [Lenawee County] Population 7,500. Named after the famous Indian leader of the early 1800s. Southeast Lower Peninsula.

telegraph- an invention to send electrical messages along wires. A telegraph operator used a switch called a key to send the messages. Telegraphs used a code made of dots and dashes to represent letters in words. The telegraph was common before the telephone or radio was widely used.

territory- land that belongs to a country but is not an official state of that country.

thumb (of Michigan)- refers to the eastern section of the Lower Peninsula which sticks out into Lake Huron. This area is known for growing sugar beets and beans.

toboggan (tah BOG an)- a long, flat-bottomed light sled made of thin boards curved up at the end.

Toledo War (toe lee doe)- the argument between Michigan and Ohio about each state's claim to the border land including Toledo. It had to be settled before Michigan could become a state.

toll road- a road or highway which charges a fee for use.

Glossary

tomahawks (TOM ah hawks)- small metal hatchets often used in fighting by Native Americans and Europeans during the 1700s.

ton- a unit of weight equal to 2,000 pounds. A full-sized car can weigh two tons.

tourist business- a business which supplies services for people as they travel for pleasure through an area. Hotels, restaurants and resorts are all a part of the tourist business.

traditions- customs and beliefs that are passed down from parents to their children.

transportation (TRANS por tay shun)- ways of moving or carrying people and goods from one place to another. Buses, cars, airplanes and trains all provide transportation.

treaty (TREE tee)- a formal agreement made between two or more nations, governments, or countries. Often a treaty settles a problem or disagreement.

Truth, Sojourner [1797 -1883]- a former slave whose real name was Isabella Baumfree. She was born in the state of New York and later moved to Battle Creek. She traveled throughout the northern states speaking against slavery.

Underground Railroad- a system which helped escaped slaves from the states in the South. The slaves were trying to reach Canada or those states in the North which did not allow slavery. It was not underground and not a railroad. It was called underground because it was secret and a railroad because it was a way to help people go from place to place. The members used railway words like station- meaning a place to hide slaves.

Union (YOUn yun)- the northern states in the Civil War. These states were against slavery, and they did not want the southern states to start their own country.

United Auto Workers or U.A.W. - a powerful union in the auto industry. Walter Reuther and his brothers, Roy and Victor, helped start the U.A.W. in the 1930s.

United Nations- a group of countries from around the world who meet in New York City to try to solve the problems of war, starvation, and poor health.

Upper Peninsula- the northern part of Michigan which is south of Lake Superior and north of Lake Michigan. It borders the state of Wisconsin.

veto (VEE toe)- the choice of the governor or President to stop a bill from becoming a law. If a bill is vetoed by the governor or President, the lawmakers can still make it a law if they have enough votes. This is usually hard to do though.

Virginia (vir jin yah)- an eastern state in the U.S. bordered on the north by West Virginia and Maryland, and on the south by North Carolina and Tennessee. Virginia was one of the original British colonies.

vote- the process of electing a person to a political office or deciding an issue.

voting rights- the rights to vote without considering someone's sex or race, etc.

War for Independence (also American Revolution)- the war fought by the American colonies from 1775 to 1783 to gain their independence from the British (England). The colonies then formed the United States.

Our Michigan Adventure

War of 1812 - a war started by the United States in 1812 to stop the British from bothering our country. The U.S. also had hopes of taking over part of Canada. The only battles ever fought in or near Michigan were during this war.

Warren- one of Michigan's largest cities. It has about 140,000 people. Warren was started in the 1830s. It is named for a general from the American War for Independence.

Wayne, General Anthony [1745-1796]-led American soldiers against hostile tribes and the British at the Battle of "Fallen Timbers" near Toledo, Ohio. The tribes were defeated. General Wayne then made a treaty for a large part of what is now Ohio and some land in Michigan.

Wayne County (WAYN cOUn tee)- a county in the southeastern section of the Lower Peninsula. It has more people than any other Michigan county. It was named for General Anthony Wayne. It was the first county in Michigan.

West Point Academy- a military school to train army officers. The school is in the state of New York.

wigwam (wig wahm)- dome-shaped framework of poles covered with hides or tree bark used as home by some of the Native Americans.

wild rice- a tall North American plant which looks like grass. It grows in swampy places. It has a grain used for food.

Williams, G. Mennen [1911-1988]- a popular governor of Michigan from 1949-1961. He was elected six times to be governor which sets a record.

Willow Run- the location of one of the world's largest war-time operations. The federal government spent $100 million on the building and the Ford Motor Company ran the factory. The assembly line was more than one mile long and 42,000 people worked at the plant making the B-24 airplanes.

wolverine (wool ver een)- a compact powerful animal with a fierce and nasty temper. Wolverines are sometimes called skunk bears.

Woodland Indians- a general name for all the tribes in the Great Lakes area since they lived in the forests and woods.

world war- there have been two wars which were so big they are called world wars. The first world war was between 1914 and 1918. It is often shortened to WWI for World War One. The second was between 1939 and 1945. It is often shortened to WWII for World War Two. Our side fought so people can remain free and have basic human rights.

WPA or Works Progress Administration- a federal organization which created jobs for the unemployed during the Great Depression. It often put people to work doing things they did best such as writing, painting, or building, etc.

Yamasaki (yam ah sock ee), **Minoru** (min or oo)- Japanese American who worked in Detroit and designed the World Trade Center in New York. It is one of the world's tallest buildings.

Index

Index

Index